Other Books by Ruth Fishel

THE JOURNEY WITHIN: A Spiritual
Path to Recovery

Booklets

From Medication to Meditation

21-Day Affirmations Workbook

LEARNING TO LIVE IN THE NOW

6-Week Personal Plan To Recovery

Ruth Fishel

Illustrated by Bonny Van de Kamp

Health Communications, Inc.
Deerfield Beach, Florida

Ruth Fishel
SPIRITHAVEN
19 Chappaquiddick Rd.
Centerville, MA 02632

Cover design by Vicki Sommer

© 1988 Ruth Fishel
ISBN 0-932194-62-1

Published by Health Communications, Inc.
Enterprise Center
3201 S.W. 15th Street
Deerfield Beach, FL 33442

She Came To Us And I Was Touched

She came to our store quietly,
   just a few times,
   Her eyes burning deep.
   Her mouth pressed almost into a straight line,
   Except for the ends of her lips
      which turned up slightly
With the faint and gentle trace of a soft smile.

She carried her head bent a little to the side
   as if the weight of all she was carrying
      were almost too much to hold up.

She said little.

When asked how she was doing
   she said, "OK!"
A little uncertain,
A little weak,
But she said, "OK."

She shared little
But when she did
I always felt her hope
Mixed in with her pain,
Mixed in with her intensity.

I felt her determination,
A stubborn determination that she would make it.

(iv) PERSONAL PLAN

When she did smile
It was if the room lit up with love
And I felt connected with God
And a Spirituality
And a closeness
That goes beyond words

I felt touched.

She shared her hope
    And her joy
        And her love
            And her determination
                With others.

But no one felt her pain at the great depths
    it must have existed until
        she was found
            hanging
                at
                    the
                        end
                        of
                        a
                        rope.

She came to us
    just a few times
And for whatever reason
    did not . . .
        could not . . .
            chose not . . .
                to share
                    the depths of her pain.

Let us learn from her death
   to share our pain.
Let us know that all of us
   who struggle with the pain of our past
Can find freedom on earth now
And do not have to be
   tied
     in
       knots
        forever.

Let us know that everyone
   carries pain,
And that by sharing it and
   becoming free
We can open the doors for others
   to unlock their pain
    and become free,
      Free from their past,
       Free to Live.

Because we all need not let our past control our now and our future, I cannot let the death of Merna Morissette go on without my notice. I will not let her life go without sharing her story with all of you.

We need not stay stuck in our pain. We can and we must take back our power so that we can be in charge of our lives.

On August 20, 1986, just three days after Merna, for reasons she took with her, chose to give up her struggle, a touching, moving memorial service was held for her by her friends and family. Her dear friend and minister, Mitzi Hill, spoke of Merna as a beautiful, loving and giving woman of only 40 years of age, and gave us the following message:

> "Finally she has given us a gift out of her life experience which I am sure she would not want us to neglect. Pain is not to be ignored, pushed down, covered up, swept under the rug or kept to oneself.
>
> "Pain is a signal, a signal of a wound that needs to be uncovered and shared with others and so be healed through the love and the power of God both directly and through the gifts He has given to those around us."

We must acknowledge her pain so that we can heal ours. We must hear and feel and know her pain. But this is not enough. We are at choice, just as she was. Hearing and knowing and feeling are not enough. We must choose to get well. We must take the action step. We must ask for help, reach down deep within, open our mouths and begin the healing process.

Rest well, Merna. Be at peace.

With love from your friend,

Ruth

Dedication

This workbook is dedicated to the beautiful memory of Merna Morissette who could not find the right door to open in order to walk through her pain. May her death serve as a spotlight for all of us so that we may open the doors of our own dark rooms and discover the joy of living in the now.

About the Illustrator

Bonny V. Lowell was born and raised in Southern California where she studied art under Corita Kent. She also lived in Aix-En-Provence, France, where her art career continued to develop. As a teacher of calligraphy she enjoys sharing her skills in bookmaking and printing. Bonny now resides in South Natick, Massachusetts, with her husband and three sons.

Special Thanks . . .

A special thanks goes to Sandy Bierig for her support, encouragement, patience and proofreading . . . to my editor, Marie Stilkind, for making me feel so good about my writing and for affirming the importance of the work that I am doing . . . to Peter Vegso and Gary Seidler, publishers of Health Communications, Inc., for their foresight and courage in the field of addictions and recovery.

Again it has been a great joy to work with Bonny Lowell, and experience her creativity and artistic talent.

Thanks to everyone who put up with me at Serenity, Inc., while I pushed to get this workbook out.

And a very special thanks again to all those who have attended my meditation classes and workshops, who have dared to step into the unknown world of meditation, imagery, visualizations and affirmations. You who have been willing to try something very different in order to grow beyond your pain, and are living proof that these pages work, thank you for sharing all the wonderful and positive results of your efforts and for encouraging me to continue to share them with others.

Dear Gentle Reader,

Welcome to Meditation Plus!

You are about to begin a very special journey . . . the journey within. It is unique and personal and fully yours. Wherever you are in this journey at this moment is perfect because it has brought you to this new stage in your growth and recovery. And you will receive exactly what it is that you are looking for, not any more, not any less.

This particular segment of your journey is designed in six sections to be taken one each week for six weeks. Please do not rush. It should not be done in less than six weeks. If you would feel more comfortable with a longer period of time, though, that will be perfect, too. You might wish to stay on some lessons longer than others. Maybe you will find it useful to carry over some of the exercises and combine them in future weeks. That is perfectly fine, too. This is your journey so customize it to your needs and your own very special growth timetable.

Before writing this workbook, I wrote **THE JOURNEY WITHIN: A *Spiritual Path to Recovery.*** In it I explained in greater detail the subjects that are covered in this workbook. After I wrote it and continued to work successfully with people in recovery, I found that the use of written exercises was a great help for improving self-discipline. It also added enjoyment and excitement to the experiences, enhancing and accelerating self-knowledge and insights. The physical acts of writing, seeing, speaking, hearing and touching bring in the senses and help to imprint new messages throughout your mind and body and spirit. This is why I felt it so important to create this workbook for you.

I have often referred to pages in **THE JOURNEY WITHIN: A *Spiritual Path to Recovery*** so that you may find further help and information. If you can, it will be very helpful to read it at the same time that you are working here. But if you cannot, don't be concerned as this workbook is complete within itself. I do advise, though, that if you do not read it now, be sure you add it to your reading list for the future.

Try to find a time that you can spend on the workbook at the same time each day as consistently as possible. You will learn tools that will be yours for the rest of your life. You will discover the very center of who you are and will open up your channels to your Higher Power and all the powers and energies of the universe. You will continue to grow to your fullest potential and feel full of peace and love.

Please know that you cannot do meditation wrong.

With Love,

Ruth Fishel

*"When we discover the still quiet place that lies within each
of us, we can see it as a base to untangle ourselves from the
doubt, indecision, ill-health, guilt and other forms of old
programming that result in confused and defused actions."*

WomanSpirit

Beginning Your Journey

You are now ready to begin your journey on your Spiritual Path
Within. It is a gentle path. So without any further delay, let's begin.

The purpose of this workbook is to introduce you to the valuable
tools of meditation, positive creative visualization and affirmations. It
is combined in a program specifically designed for anyone who has
difficulty with addictions or compulsions, or is a co-dependent. It
would certainly be useful, however, for anyone who wishes to grow. It
is especially valuable for Adult Children of Alcoholics or Dysfunctional Families.

At the times when I have referred to alcohol, just substitute
whatever fits you so that these tools can have personal meaning in
your life.

Before you begin, please remember

You cannot do meditation wrong.

To gain the full benefits of *Meditation Plus*, a small period of time
each day is needed. To expect to grow without taking action will just
lead to frustration and eventually lack of interest. So be good to
yourself. Make a commitment to grow and develop on your Spiritual
Path so that you can know the joy of living and develop your personal
power.

Take your time. Make a set time for yourself every day. Try to have
a set place where you know your privacy will be respected.

In the following weeks, we will cover the points listed next. If any
title jumps out and calls to you, by all means turn to that first.
Otherwise, I suggest that you take them in order.

Contents

The following is the basic plan for the journey you will be on for the next six weeks. Each session will cover the points listed. Please remember that if you wish to go more slowly, please do. Follow your own inclinations on this. Trust yourself. But do not rush to finish it in less than six weeks. This path cannot be rushed. It is your personal path to recovery.

Week 1

Week 2

Week 3

Week 4

Week 5

Week 6

Week 1

Personal Plan
For Meditation Plus

This first week will introduce you to the basics of meditation. Again, remember that you can take your own time and do this as slowly as you like. Trust yourself. It is your personal path to recovery. It cannot be done wrong.

Values Of Meditation

Before going any further, it is important for you to know how valuable meditation is and all the results that you can gain from meditating.

Meditation is simply a
Quieting Down of Thoughts
A Settling Down of the Mind
Awareness
Insight

Here are other values to be gained with meditation:

* Lowers blood pressure and heart rate.
* Helps release energy blocked by stress, anxiety, worry, fear, guilt, anger, blame and depression.
* Reduces stress, anxiety, worry, fear and all the other factors that block us from realizing our full potential.
* Helps to discover deeper meaning in everyday experiences.
* Helps to get in touch with our Universal Energy, and teaches us how to *tap into that power at all times.*
* Releases old tapes. Helps us to become "unstuck".
* Reduces blocks that keep us resisting change so that we can begin to take responsibility for our own lives by letting us know we are at choice at all times.
* Increases mastery over attention.
* Improves overall health.
* You will learn to come to peace with yesterday and give up the fear of tomorrow.
* Discover the power that comes from knowing that you are at choice at all times.

Discover Your Inner Power
Remember . . . It Is Impossible To Do
Meditation Wrong
You Cannot Fail

"You will reach down into your mind to a new place of safety. You will recognize you have reached it if you find a sense of deep peace . . . however briefly. Let go of all trivial things that churn and bubble on the surface of your mind, and reach down below them. There is a place in you where there is perfect peace . . . There is a place in you where nothing is impossible . . . There is a place in you where the strength of God . . . Your Higher Power . . . lives."

Adapted from A Course of Miracles

Basic Description Of Course

Once you begin on this path, you will not want to stop. You have been walking in darkness too long. Lights will begin to go on for you and show you your truth.

You will get in touch with the blocks that keep you from being the terrific person you are.

Many of us have preconceived ideas of what meditation is. Maybe in our mind's eye we picture someone sitting yoga style, body erect, in a white robe for hours and hours.

The meditation we will do is based in Buddhism and is called Vipassana Meditation. It is a very simple meditation that will teach you single-pointed concentration and insight. It goes back over 2500 years to the time of the Buddha, and is also known as Insight Meditation or Mindfulness.

Vipassana Meditation consists of the traditional sitting meditation. It also consists of a walking meditation to help us to learn awareness and concentration. It is a tool to learn to live in the now, to become aware, to become insightful during all the hours of the day. It will help us to get in touch with a Power greater than ourselves, to find peace and serenity, and to help us first to accept and then to love ourselves.

Meditation is an important tool for self-knowledge. It will enable us to see ourselves as we really are and allow us to let go of our character defects so that we can move ahead.

In the **Twelve Steps and Twelve Traditions** from Alcoholics Anonymous, World Service, Inc., it states:

"When we refuse air, light and food, the body suffers. And when we turn away from meditation and prayer, we likewise deprive our minds, our emotions and our intuitions of vitally needed support. As the body can fail its purpose for lack of nourishment, so can the soul."

And it goes on to say that "there is a direct linkage between self-examination, meditation and prayer." It says . . .

"Meditation is our step into the sun"

It is, important, therefore, to remember that while we are learning to meditate in a sitting position, while paying attention to our breathing, we are beginning to learn mindfulness. We will gain insight into our true nature.

The Power Of Positive Thought

We are also going to learn how powerful our minds are; that we have the power and ability to turn around our negative thinking into positive thinking for positive results in our lives. We will learn that we are not victims of the universe. We will see that we no longer need to let persons, places or things control us.

Positive Creative Visualization

Visualizations are excellent tools to use to turn around the negative tapes you often hear and see into positive ones. They can help you begin to move toward becoming the fulfilled person that you want to be. You can create new goals and actually visualize yourself already achieving them in your mind. By creating a positive new picture in your mind and then letting your body actually experience the feeling as if it has actually happened, you will be able to create new positive experiences with more and more ease.

Used regularly, visualizations can be powerful tools to help us act in new ways. As we will learn later in this book, our bodies cannot discern the difference between real and imagined situations. They will believe what our minds imagine, thereby responding to real or imagined situations in exactly the same way.

Visualizations are like dress rehearsals. If you imagine a situation often enough, then by the time that you actually find yourself in that situation, it will be familiar to you. For example, if you imagine that you have confidence in a future situation, your body will respond with confidence when it occurs. If you do this often enough, you can form new habits so that your mind and your body will respond as you choose in any actual situation.

Affirmations

Affirmations are another powerful tool for changing negative tapes into positive ones. Used daily, you will find that an entire new attitude will lead to a positive and wonderful way of life.

An affirmation is a positive thought that we imagine as if it were true in the now. If we say it and feel it with conviction, it will become true. An affirmation can be written or stated positively. But if we write our affirmation and then read it aloud, we are using our eyes, our ears and our bodies to affirm the new messages we are telling ourselves.

As in visualization, affirmations are stated as if they were happening now, as if they were real. They affirm your visualization. They work when they are said with *conviction*, stated as if they are true in the *now*, are said with *energy* and are *repeated* at least 10 times a day for 21 days. A few examples of affirmations that might be helpful for you are:

I deserve to let good things happen in my life today.

I am moving towards the right job for me.

I am meeting people who are positive and supportive in my life.

Basic Sitting Meditation Instructions

How To Dress

Wear comfortable, loose clothing. Be sure it is appropriate for the weather. You will soon be sitting for a long time, and it will be best to dress so that you are not conscious of warmth or cold.

How To Sit

Where you sit is less important than how you sit. It is important to have your back and your neck straight and your chin slightly up.

If you can sit yoga style with your legs crossed, in a lotus or semi-lotus position, you will have the best balance for longer periods of sitting. At first this may seem very uncomfortable and your body might not want to sit that way. You may wish to get a book of yoga exercises and learn how to stretch your body so that it can be comfortable in that position. The more you try it, the easier it will get.

If you cannot learn the lotus or the semi-lotus, you can sit cross-legged, Indian-style.

It can be very helpful in any of these positions to sit on a pillow with your legs on the floor for better balance.

If you find that you cannot manage this position, you can sit in a chair with your feet flat on the floor. Be sure your back and your neck are straight and your chin is slightly down.

The Perfect Place

"The happiness of solitude is not found in retreats. It may be had even in busy centers. Happiness is not to be sought in solitude or in busy centers. It is in the self."
Sri Ramana Maharshi

There are basically three types of places to meditate.

First, there is inside your home where you spend much of your time. If this is in a family setting, try to find time for yourself when it is most quiet. Ask that this time be respected by all and that you are not interrupted. Know that you are not asking for any special favors. You are not more special than the other members of the family, but you deserve this time just as others deserve it.

It might be necessary to get up earlier than the rest of the family. (If you think that this will be difficult for you to do, read the section on setting your personal clock.) You will be amazed at the ease and joy you will receive in being in charge of your own time.

If your current home is shared with others who are not your family, such as a hospital, treatment center, halfway house or group home, the same suggestions as stated above apply to you here. It might be more of a challenge to find that quiet time, but it can be done if you want it.

Also know that you do not have to meditate alone. It can be a very beautiful, powerful experience to meditate with a roommate, a spouse, a lover, a friend or a group of people, just as long as all involved are committed to peace and quiet in meditation.

Meditation can be done outside . . . at the beach or in the woods or in your own backyard. Often it is not the most quiet spot because noises that are absolutely out of your control, such as squirrels, birds, crashing waves, strong winds, etc., can be very disturbing. But if you are concentrated enough to just let these noises be, this also can be a most rewarding experience.

Second, meditating with a group while taking lessons is usually a more controlled environment where noises are at a minimum and the space is comfortable. This is a good way to learn and a good way to practice, but it is important to realize that this controlled environment cannot always be duplicated at home. If you expect it, disappointments will occur. There is often more power found when meditating with a group.

Third is the experience of meditating at a retreat where the conditions are designed to be as perfect as possible. We need to know that it is not practical to expect to duplicate them in real life. When we return to the reality of our everyday lives, we need to learn how to be in charge of our own time and our own space and accept the reality of our present conditions.

Experiencing Meditation By Following Your Breath

Now sit comfortably again and relax. If someone can read this to you it would be most helpful! But if you are doing this by yourself, that is fine, too. Just read this over first and then follow the instructions. You might need to read them a few times, but they are simple and you will get used to them.

Close your eyes and begin to breathe in and breathe out. Don't try to control your breathing in any way. Just let it be natural.

Get To Know The Characteristics Of Your Breath

For the next two or three minutes, just close your eyes and sit quietly and be aware of your breathing.

Be aware of your breath as it goes in and as it goes out of your nose. Don't follow your breath all the way down or control or force your breathing. In the beginning it helps to make mental notes of "rising/falling" or "in/out". This aids in keeping your mind on your breathing.

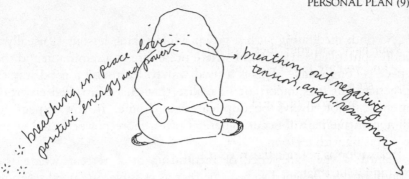

breathing in peace love positive energy and power

breathing out negative tension, anger, resentment

Just notice your breath, as it goes in and as it goes out. See if you can notice if it is cool or warm, long or short. Don't try to make it something that it is not. Don't change it. Just let it be and observe it. Notice if it is shallow or deep. Notice if it changes.

If thoughts come in, just let them be and go back to your breathing.

If feelings come up, just notice them and go back to your breathing.

If you experience an itch or a pain, try not to move. Bring your attention to that area of your body and watch it as it changes and moves away.

If you get lost in a thought or a daydream, just notice that you got lost and bring your attention back to your breathing. It would be helpful to make a mental note of what it was that took you away from your breathing.

Now plan to spend a few more moments experiencing meditation.

Let your body relax.

Feel relaxation flow through your head
   and your neck.

Relax your eyes
   and your mouth
     and your face.

Feel tension leave the back of your neck
   and your shoulders.

Let relaxation pour down your arms
   and your hands
     and tension flow out through your
       fingers.

Your back and your chest are relaxing
   and you are feeling relaxation in your
      stomach
         and your hips and
            your pelvis.

Relaxation is pouring down your hips
   and your thighs
      and your knees.

Your legs are feeling so relaxed
   as are your ankles
      and your feet
         and your toes.

Now go back and check your body for any left-over
   tightness and bring relaxation to them.

And then return your attention to your
   breathing
      as you breathe in
         and you breathe out . . .
            as you breathe in
               and you breathe out.

Know that as you breathe in,
   you are breathing in positive energy.
      You are breathing in power
         and love
            and good.

And as you breath out you are exhaling
   all the negative elements that block you
      from your Higher Power.

You are breathing out tension
   and anger
      and resentments.

Breathe in and breathe out . . .

Breathe in
   and breathe out.

Now just be with your breathing for a while . . .

And when you are ready, count to five very slowly before opening your eyes and come back to the room.

It Is Absolutely Normal To Have Thoughts

Just notice them and go back to your breathing.

Notice your thoughts and return to your breathing.

Bring your attention back to your breathing.

If you notice yourself planning for something in the future, just notice it and go back to your breathing.

If you notice that you are letting in a past memory, just notice that and return to your breathing.

There Will Always Be Noises

As with thoughts, just notice the noises and go back to your breathing. Don't try to block them out. Don't resist them. Just hear them and bring your attention back to your breathing.

Notice . . . Don't Resist Or Struggle

Whatever comes up for you, just let it be and go back to your breathing. The more you practice this, the easier it will become.

The more you struggle with a thought, the more it will stay in your mind and take over. You will see that if you just notice it, it will gradually disappear.

Spend a good 10 or 15 minutes with this exercise and then very gradually open your eyes and return to the room.

How Long To Practice
Sitting Meditation

It is important to remember that we are learning a very simple meditation based on a Buddha Meditation called Vipassana or Insight Meditation, and that it is more than sitting meditation. It is a meditation to gain insight. It is a meditation to gain awareness.

To meditate just once in a while will have little if any value. But if you begin to practice it on a daily basis, you will find extraordinary results. You can discover *healthy and natural* highs and good feelings that you looked for in alcohol and drugs or other dependencies. And, most important, you will begin to know that there really is a terrific person living inside you after all, someone you just have not yet had the privilege of meeting.

Begin with as little as 10 minutes in the morning and, if possible, 10 minutes at night. You can gradually increase this as you are able. As few as 10 minutes a day done on a daily basis will produce results.

How To Return From
Meditations And Visualizations

When you meditate, you are at a deeper level of consciousness. Your breathing, heart rate, pulse and blood pressure have all slowed down to the equivalent of sleep. It can be very jarring to just open your eyes and immediately resume moving around. Headaches and irritability can result.

When you are ready, return to the room; but always come back very slowly. Never open your eyes until you have counted to at least five. It is helpful to prepare yourself to come back by picturing the room that you are in and picturing yourself in the room.

If coming out of meditation is outside of your control, such as being disturbed by an unexpected noise like a doorbell or telephone ring, try to return to meditation for at least five minutes. That extra five minutes may make the difference between a relaxing, peaceful day or one of irritability and stress.

Remember, in all ways be gentle with yourself . . . including your return to consciousness!

Learning To Be In The Now

You will find a great value in this kind of meditation for a slowing down, a relaxation and a beginning to see how your mind works *from moment to moment.*

There are exercises later which will help you to experience your *now.*

When we were into escaping, looking outside ourselves for happiness, it was impossible to know what we were experiencing in the *now* because our *now* was not real! *We were never in the now! We chose our addiction or escape instead of reality.*

You are learning to be in charge of your mind.

You are learning to experience the present.

You are learning to choose the reality of the now and live.

*You will find your strength within you
in places deep inside where you have
not yet dared to visit.
Know that you have all that you need
to do all that is good and right in your life today.*

Relaxation Symbols

When you take time to do your regular daily meditations, you can use the process you have learned on basic meditation to bring relaxation through your entire body and quiet your mind.

There will be other times that you will want to go into your special place or just relax so that you can do visualizations and affirmations without meditating first. It will be necessary to feel relaxed so that these exercises can be as effective as possible.

Once you get used to the process of meditation, it will become easier and easier to relax at will. For example, if you are standing in line in the bank, late for an appointment and feel yourself becoming irritated and uptight at your apparent powerlessness in the situation, you can bring your attention to your breathing and relax. As you bring your attention to your breath, as it goes in and goes out of your nose, you can feel peace and relaxation flow through your entire body. You get into a new habit of responding with relaxation when you bring your attention to your breath.

Another way of relaxing at will is to visualize a symbol that means relaxation to you. For example, a gently soaring seagull flying high in the sky or a sailboat drifting on the distant horizon. One person I know uses a waterfall.

Find a symbol that makes you feel peaceful.

Close your eyes and let yourself picture that symbol.

Let peace and relaxation flow through your entire
body.

Feel the peace.

Know the peace.

Enjoy the peace.

Keep this symbol for as long as you want it. Change it or vary it whenever you wish. The main point is that it will take you to a state of relaxation that works for you.

Your mind will be able to picture this symbol with greater ease the more you use it. As your mind pictures your symbol, your body will begin to respond automatically by relaxing itself more and more quickly as you continue this practice. There will soon come a time when all you will need to do is picture your symbol and your body will almost simultaneously become relaxed. This is not only very valuable for all the exercises here, but for all the stress in your life as well.

"Peace and relaxation flow through me with every breath that I take."

MY SPECIAL VISUALIZATION SYMBOL

Date _____

The more that you can visualize your symbol in your mind, the greater impression it will make on your subconscious.

Picture your symbol in your mind and draw it as best as you can. It does not have to be perfect. Just draw your idea of your symbol. If it is of something that is common, why not look through a few magazines and see if you can find a picture of it. If you can, then just cut it out and paste it here to add to your visual image.

My Symbol Is (one word or full description) ———————————

——————————————————————————————

——————————————————————————————

——————————————————————————————

——————————————————————————————

Draw or paste picture of symbol here.

Introduction To Your Inner Sanctuary

". . . As long as we stand outside,
we are outsiders."

D.T. Suzuki

There is a very special place inside each and every one of us. It is a place where we are perfectly safe, a place where we find peace. It is where the very core of existence lies, where our truth lives. It's that special place we talked about earlier that has been buried throughout the years where our spark of energy, life and love lives.

Over all these years our need to fulfill our longings and desires has caused us to reach outward rather than inward. As we took more and more of what was out there, we found that it helped us less and less and we became addicts or co-dependents or both.

It was very natural that if we felt "less than", we would want to fill up with "more" to feel better. But the process of filling up cannot happen until we first empty. And we cannot empty until we see what has to be emptied. And we cannot see what has to be emptied until we put a light on in our dark room.

Begin To Use Your Recipe

1. *Bring quiet to your mind*
2. *Begin to know yourself by using all your senses*

Meditation is your tool to look within. Meditation is your tool to quiet your mind long enough to begin to put a light on in your dark room. Meditation is your tool to quiet your mind to begin your journey home to self-awareness, self-knowledge and wisdom.

Know that you are not alone on your special journey within and that you will soon know that you never have to be alone again. You are being led by a power greater than yourself. As you open more and more to the energies of the universe, you will find your inner or true self.

You will go home to your very source. This path to your source has to be traveled so that you can be in the here and now.

You will not be sorry. It is what you have waited for and looked for all your life. All the time that you have been reaching out, your answers were within you. All the time that you were trying this or that, here or there, this person or that person, your answers for peace and serenity were no further away than your own breath.

breathing
in ∴ out
↑
that marvelous space

Special Meditation To Go Into Your Inner Sanctuary

Get yourself into a comfortable position. Begin to relax. Close your eyes gently and begin to bring your attention to your breathing. Bring to mind your relaxation symbol. Now spend a few minutes following your meditation routine.

Take some time to think about how you would design a perfect place for yourself. It can be anywhere and made out of anything. It can be inside or out of doors, made of any material that you choose, and of any design that makes you happy.

Create a place where you are perfectly safe, where you feel really good about yourself. Know that nothing can happen to you in this place that you do not want to have happen. This is your place . . . just for you. No one else can enter it unless you invite them.

As you begin to feel relaxed, let yourself go deep within.

Let yourself go deep within

    to this very special, quiet place inside.

Let yourself go

    deep within

        to your very special place

            where you are completely safe.

This is your special place . . . your inner sanctuary.

Take some time to use all your senses to know your place. Are there any special sounds? Any special aromas? How does it feel beneath your fingers and beneath your feet? What time of the year is it? What time of day? Is it warm or cold?

Know that you can come here any time you wish.

Know that you can change it any time you wish . . . add to it . . . change the scenery . . . the furniture . . . the time of year . . . the time of day.

Know that this is your special safe place where you can be alone to learn about yourself and find peace.

"It feels so safe to know that there is always a special place within me where I can feel peace."

Warning!

Meditation may be positive for your health.

If you don't want to feel better . . . stop reading.

It is important for you to know it is a law of the universe that the more you put into something, the more you take out of it. To meditate once a week and expect miracles would truly be a miracle. But to meditate daily and begin to take action will guarantee results.

The actual formal time spent on meditation daily is infinitesimal in comparison to the results that you will experience.

Follow this simple suggestion and noticeable, positive changes will begin to occur for you within three to seven days.

Personal Prescription For First Week

Be Gentle With Yourself . . .

1. Meditation

Begin with a minimum of 10 to 20 minutes each morning and each night. If you find that you choose to meditate only once each day, make that one meditation in the morning. This will help you get into the right frame of mind for your full 24 hours.

2. Awareness

Begin to bring awareness to everything you do. Do not judge anything that comes up. Just bring awareness. Notice yourself. Get to know yourself. Start to know who you are and what makes you tick without judgment. This is the beginning of the process of self-acceptance and self-love.

As you begin to develop the regular habit of meditation, you will begin to hear the conversations that continually take place in your mind. You will begin to become aware of your *self-talk*, the things that you tell yourself. You will begin to hear negative tapes and how they reinforce a poor self-image. And you will gradually begin to learn that these negative tapes that come from your past experiences are deeply embedded in your subsconscious and keep you stuck from moving forward.

As Henry Ford once said,

"Whether you think you can or can't, you're right!"

Learning To Be In The Now

You will find great value in this kind of meditation for slowing down as a relaxation and as a beginning to see how your mind works.

Select one habitual experience that you do everyday, such as washing dishes, brushing your teeth or showering. Bring your full attention to that experience.

For example, if you select brushing your teeth, bring your full attention to the sounds of the water in the sink and the toothbrush in your mouth. Smell the toothpaste. Feel the sensations as you brush.

And as your mind begins to wander, notice what takes you away from the *now*, from the *moment* and what you are doing in the moment. Do not judge, but learn from what you see. Notice whether you are letting past thoughts or feelings rob you of your now. Or does future planning and worrying keep coming in? Maybe fear or guilt or anxiety takes you away from *being alive in the moment*.

Just notice what is happening. And jot down what comes up as BLOCKS.

REMEMBER . . .

**You can't do meditation wrong.
Wherever you are is perfect.**

"I am beginning to learn who I am right now without judgment and with love and acceptance."

Commitment

I will meditate a minimum of 10 minutes at least one, but preferably two, times a day.

I will bring my full attention to the following habit or routine that I do daily _____ .

Observations

I have made the following new discoveries as a result of this commitment:

Reflecting On Personal Goals

Date _____

This is a good time to stop and rest a while, letting all that you have read settle in and become a part of you.

Spend a few minutes getting in touch with your breath.

Slow down and be gentle with yourself.

Now take a few moments and think about what you would like to get out of this next six weeks.

1. What are your goals?

2. What would you like to change? Where would you like to let go?

3. What would you like to add to your life?

Think a few moments and jot down some answers. Write down whatever comes up for you first. You don't have to wait until you get it perfect, grammatically or any other way. Remember, this is your journey and no one else will see this unless you invite them to.

First Week Checklist

It is so easy to begin a new project with excitement and enthusiasm. Then within a few days, if you don't see immediate results (and sometimes even if you do), boredom sets in. The initial energy and enthusiasm wears off. You are apt to forget or other demands tend to fill up that space. It is so easy to say *yes* to others, and *I am too busy* when it comes to doing things for ourselves. Therefore a commitment checklist can often help with *self-discipline*.

You will find that these exercises soon become habits and you will do them as automatically as brushing your teeth. Add anything else you would like to do regularly to this list.

	Mon	Tues	Wed	Thur	Fri	Sat	Sun
Morning Meditation							
Morning Inspirational Readings							
Attention to One Routine							
Evening Inspirational Readings							
Evening Meditation							

Week 2

Personal Plan
For Meditation Plus

If you have been following the instructions for the week, you are definitely beginning to notice a big change in your attitude and energy. Chances are you feel more calm more often and new awarenesses are beginning to surface.

Remember, this is not a guarantee to feel wonderful all the time. It is a guarantee that if you follow these simple instructions, you will be able to cope with all that happens in your life with increasingly greater ease and overall happiness.

It is important to remember to follow your own comfortable pace. Refer back to the first week as often as you like.

Writing Second Week's Experiences

Date _____

Before beginning your second week of meditation, spend some time reflecting on what you may have noticed going on for you this week. As you begin to bring your awareness to all that is going on around you, little lights of "AHA!" and "OH, NO!" insights can be relatively commonplace.

Remember, when thoughts come in and out as you are doing your sitting meditation, you just notice them and do not judge them and treat all your other awarenesses with the same respect. Just notice them and do not judge them.

Take a few minutes to reflect and explore thoughts and feelings and insights. Here are a few questions that you might ask yourself to get started.

1. How did I respond to the variety of feelings that came up during meditation, ie, calmness, agitation, impatience, boredom, happiness, fear, etc?

2. Did I feel different this week?

3. When I brought my attention to one routine, I . . .

4. I accomplished more _____ less _____ same _____ this week.

5. I learned these new things about me . . .

6. I felt better _____ worse _____ same _____ about myself.

7. Important points to remember:

Now go on with your own questions . . . exploring . . .
thinking . . . re-feeling.

Pause For Reflections

Date _____

The Power Of Our Minds

We will now do some exercises on the power of our minds, and gain understanding of how we are at choice and responsible for our lives.

We will learn that . . .

We are our thoughts.

What we think we create.

We choose who we are.

We create our chaos as well as our balance.

We are at choice at all times.

Everything New Begins In The Mind

Everything that is created begins in the mind. An author's imagination plans a book before it is written. An architect does the plans for a building mentally before putting them on paper. All pictures and plays and cartoons, etc., all begin with a single thought.

Our minds are very powerful. What we see in our minds can affect the way our bodies feel. Let's try a few examples:

Close your eyes very gently and picture a big lemon. Picture cutting the lemon in half with a knife. In your mind feel the sides of the lemon with your fingers. Feel the rough surface. Now take that half of the lemon and put it in your mouth. Let yourself stay with that picture for a few minutes as your lips and tongue stay in contact with the lemon.

Now picture something else that you can drink or eat to take away the sour taste of the lemon. Put that in your mouth instead and feel the difference.

Some people cannot visualize pictures at first. They have a stronger sense of knowing or feeling or smelling. Do not let this worry you if you cannot actually see a picture. That will come in time and with practice. In the meantime, use any sense that is the strongest for you so that you can experience the visualizations.

Now picture that you are driving in a car. It is early evening and the road is empty and you have the music on the radio. You are very relaxed. Everything is peaceful. Suddenly a dog runs out from nowhere and is almost in front of your car. You slam on the brakes and swerve, avoiding the dog by inches. You sit there for a few minutes, grateful that you missed the animal but conscious of all the feelings that went on in your body because of this near miss.

Thoughts Tell Our Bodies How To Respond

It is now time for you to be in charge of those feelings. Visualizations are a way to change being controlled by old, negative feelings.

Remember, we act out who we think we are and we can feel physically what our minds tell us to feel.

"Someday, after we have mastered the winds, the waves, the tides and the gravity, we shall harness for God the energies of love. Then, for the second time in the history of the world, man will have discovered fire."

Teilhard de Chardin

I believe that deep within every human being lies the true essence of our being, a spark of life and love, a pure spark of energy that gives us all our sameness. Each experience thereafter establishes our uniqueness.

Each moment and experience of life after birth either kindles or covers this spark. But no matter what we experience, even if we can no longer feel this spark, no matter how many layers and layers of negative experiences have covered and buried our spark of life, it can never be completely extinguished.

Love, kindness, caring, touching and gentleness nurtures and stokes this spark into a warm and constant glow. Those of us who have had the good fortune to be brought up in such an atmosphere are truly lucky human beings.

Some have been fortunate enough to have been born to two normal, loving, intelligent, financially secure parents. These parents loved and gave their children discipline and encouragement. Their children were held and touched and felt loved, and then they could give love back. They were taught to be independent, self-sufficient and highly motivated. They were taught about morals and standards and that life was about love. Growing up under these loving circumstances stoked that tiny spark. These children grew up to be trusting people, capable of giving and receiving love naturally and easily.

. . . And then there are the rest of us!!!

The rest of us were also born with this tiny spark of love and life. And to oversimplify our upbringing just to make a point, the alternatives to the ideal upbringing just described could be:

1) deprivation of love

or

2) inconsistent conditional love

or

3) grey areas of both.

Most of us fit into number 3.

> *Insanity is repeating the same things over and over again,*
> *and expecting different results.*

our negative past put
layers and layers over
our spark

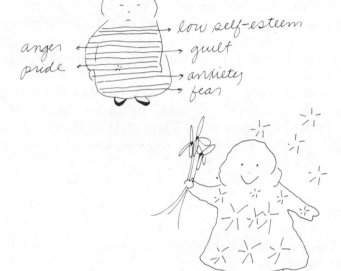

low self-esteem

anger
pride

guilt

anxiety
fear

begin the process of removing
the old layers to
discover your real self!

It's like the story of the Princess and the Pea, but in reverse. If you remember, the Princess was so sensitive that even when she slept on 20 mattresses, she could still feel the pea that was under the bottom one.

Well, we were so desensitized because of all the negative experiences and we had put up so many walls, we could no longer feel our spark of love. We had to begin the process of removing each layer so we could get back to who we really were.

Turning Stumbling Blocks
Into Stepping Stones

*"Today I have the courage to look without fear at
what needs to be changed in my life."*

"You are going to find a star to light your path."

A Course of Miracles

a star is lighting your path

*"We cannot leave the trap until we know that we are in it.
We are in a needless imprisonment."*

Marilyn Ferguson

The Dark Room

*"It is more practical to light a candle than to
curse the darkness."*

Chinese Proverb

Until we are ready to look within to heal and grow, we have
absolutely no chance of ever getting better. Until we are ready to give
up playing the *"IF"* game or the *"WHEN"* game, the *BLAME* game,
we will stay in pain. Until we stop saying and thinking things like "If
only she would understand me . . ." or "If only we had more
money . . ." or "When I finish college, it will be better." Until we stop
looking to later or someone or something, we remain blocked.

Imagine living in one big dark black room, constantly groping
around to try to find your way around. Imagine bumping into things
and moving away, then suddenly finding a clear spot where you could
walk for a while. But there would soon be something else looming
before you again and you would be hurt once more.

If you are wearing heavy armor, you won't feel it when you bump
into things, but the armor will become more and more dented as time
goes on so that it will work for you less and less effectively.

Now imagine taking off the armor and simply turning a light on in
this room so that you can actually see the obstacles that have been in
your way. You can see each item and move it before walking into it
and getting bruised again.

This is similar to what is going on inside of you that is blocking your
way to freedom. Until you are able to shine a light on your stumbling
blocks, you will remain stuck in the darkness of your pain. And if you
have been drinking and drugging, chances are you have blocked your
ability to feel. So when you finally stop reaching for the drug to feel
better, you will begin to feel your pain. You will finally be able to deal
with it.

You are once again at a place in your path called *choices.*

If your choice is for freedom and growth . . .

A STAR IS LIGHTING YOUR PATH! KEEP GOING!

Once you see the obstacles in your dark room, you will discover that there is a door. And you have the key.

And that key is Willingness.

And you can use these blocks for stepping stones to go on with your life.

Self-Talk

"Our own creative energy is waiting to move through us once we get out of our own way. Cleansing the mind of negative thought, quieting the chatterer and becoming one with the moment provides the environment for this energy to flow through us."

Ruth Ross

As you go further into the practice of meditation, you will begin to notice more and more of what goes on inside your head. You will soon become aware as you never have before, of the endless conversations, observations, judgments, opinions and projections that constantly happen in your mind. You will become aware that the longer you allow this to happen, that you will not always be comfortable with this endless activity. You will see that it was often this very unrest that sent you running away before into your addiction.

Now, by allowing yourself to experience your inner conversations, your "self-talk", you will soon begin to know yourself on a new level. You will be able to observe how you react, experience, feel and think. The longer you practice and the more that you really listen, the more clearly you will see who you really are.

You will begin to hear the "self-talk" that has influenced you throughout your entire life, without you even knowing it. You will finally begin to shine a light on the tapes that have come from old experiences, other people and other places and have absolutely no value in your life today.

And as you learn to meditate at a deeper level, you will begin to learn the sources of this "self-talk." So you will learn how to change it into a positive factor in your life today. In the quiet of your meditation, you will learn to observe it at a detached level. The more that you can see and hear, the more that you can accept. And as you gently accept the truth about yourself, old tapes will begin to lose their power over you. Their noise will gradually diminish. You will learn to take charge of your mind and you will become free.

Staying With It No Matter What

It is important to notice here how natural it is for you to want to run away or escape. Every time you have given in to this urge in the past, you have buried your truth more deeply. Stay with it, be with it, go through it and learn from it, no matter what!

At times your self-talk might become painful. Self-talk has been taped from old messages. As you begin to isolate old tapes, and this is a very important point for you to realize, you will become clearer about your conscious mind's conversations with itself. You might hear messages like the following:

"You're not good enough."

"You'll never amount to anything."

"Hurry up! There's more to do."

"There will never be enough for all of us."

"I'll never get what I need."

"Why bother? There will be smarter and more experienced people applying."

When you begin to hear that these are the messages that have blocked you from moving forward in many areas of your life, when you start to see that these messages and many like them came from times you might not like to remember in your past, your first impulse might be never to meditate again.

And the more painful the messages and memories are, the more desire you will have to relieve that pain. But remember, truth has always been blocked by your escaping into your addiction before. Just one drink or one pill or one bite won't help. Hiding is no longer an option if you want to live.

The truth is not gone because your eyes are closed.

But more often than not, self-talk is not painful, but fascinating! As you begin to hear the constant chatter that takes place in your mind, you will begin to understand many things. One will be the way you fail to hear all of the other person's conversation. You might notice that while someone else is talking, you are planning ahead to what you are going to say. Or your eye might have been caught by something interesting and your mind is off and running and speculating about it.

Our minds are constantly chattering away, judging this, criticizing that, blaming this, praising that . . . commenting, commenting, commenting.

*It is a proven fact that you cannot have two thoughts
in your mind at the same time.*

One way to stop negative or tiring self-talk is to breathe in *peace*
with each in-breath. You can vary this with the word *love*.

Breathe in *peace*

and breathe out anxiety

very gently.

Breathe in *peace*

and breathe out thoughts

very gently.

This also works very well if you are having difficulty falling asleep.
This is a very simple routine to do.

*releasing the worry cycles
thru meditation*

Dr. Herbert Benson, in his excellent book **Beyond The Relaxation Response,** refers to this phenomenon as "loops" formed in the "wiring" of your brain and says that by focusing your thinking on word, sound, prayer or exercise, the chain of everyday worrisome thought is broken. He calls these mental patterns, these unproductive grooves or circuits that cause the mind to "play" over and over again, almost involuntarily, the same anxieties or health-impairing thoughts, "worry cycles".

Simply explained, these "worry cycles" create anxiety and stress. Meditation counteracts the harmful effects by relaxing our mind and our bodies.

Exercise To Help You See The Effect Of Your Self-Talk

Exercise 1

Whatever we think, we feel

Words are very powerful. What we think in our minds, responds in our bodies. When we relive old experiences, our bodies do not know whether they are happening now or in our minds, so our bodies respond as if it were now. When we project into the future and picture ourselves in any experience, our bodies respond as if it were happening now. Our minds and our bodies do not know the difference between real and imagined.

As we learn to quiet our minds by meditation, we are more able to see and hear the messages we give ourselves. Once we begin to see and hear, then we can change.

When you are no longer drinking or drugging, when you no longer reach out to persons, places and things to find your inner peace and happiness. when you are no longer dulling your senses with everything but the truth, you will begin to hear your own self-talk. Begin to look at your self-talk. Are your words from your personal conversations and the conversations that go on in your head, your self-talk, negative or positive?

Notice the effect your self-talk has on your body. Begin to *feel* how

judgmental self-talk

your mind becomes free to really listen

your body responds to words and events. Begin to *experience* how you can change this effect on yourself.

Listen to your self-talk without judgment. Notice your self-talk as if you were watching two people in a movie. You are just noticing a conversation going on, hearing it and learning from it. See the section on self-talk for further reading. This is another step on your journey to becoming gentle with yourself . . . to becoming softer and happier and more relaxed. Remember . . . you deserve peace. You deserve love. You deserve freedom and happiness.

As you begin to hear your self-talk in your internal and external conversations, start taking note of the words you find yourself using. Write them down in the column where they belong. Remember, this is how we brighten the light in our dark room. We cannot stop from stumbling and continuing to give ourselves pain if we do not take the time to put a light on and see what it is we are stumbling into in the dark.

"It is so freeing to know that I am no longer controlled by the voices that go in my head."

Recording My Self-Talk

Beginning Date _____

Positive Words   **Negative Words**

Self-Talk

Exercise 2

"Words give rise to all our feelings. Whatever we think and feel, we think and feel through the power of words. Through words we experience the duality between pleasure and pain, good and evil, virtue and sin. If someone calls you a sinner, you feel insulted and ashamed. But if someone calls you a good person, you become happy. This is the duality created by words, and because of this duality you suffer or experience happiness."

Swami Muktananda

Words are just as powerful when they come from someone else. Until we reprogram our own self-talk and grow in our own personal self-esteem, what other people say to us will directly affect how we feel about ourselves. We originally received our inner messages from those around us in earliest childhood. Remember that our earliest messages were how we judged ourselves, how we knew if we were okay or loved or worthwhile. They came from outside in, and the more they were repeated, the more strongly we owned them. They became imprinted in our subconscious to be heard over and over again.

Become another kind of a listener now. Listen to the words of others and feel how they affect you. Notice how you react if someone talks down to you or looks at you in any way but loving and complimentary. Jot down how other people's looks and gestures and words affect you.

Notice, too, how you are as a listener. As you hear others talk to you, what does your self-talk do? Is it quiet while you listen? Is it respectful? Or does it judge the other person, questioning whether the truth is being said. For example, if someone tells you that you look good today, might you say to yourself: "I wonder why she said that?" Or do you think about what you want to say next and, therefore, are not really listening to the full conversation.

- How do you react to compliments?
- How do you take criticism?

- What happens in your body if you are confronted or someone is angry with you?
- What does it feel like to have someone say: "I love you?"

These are just a few of the questions you can begin to ask yourself as you observe yourself as a listener.

How I Am Affected By What Others Say

Beginning Date _____

"To study the way is to study the self.
To study the self is to forget the self.
To forget the self is to be enlightened by all things.
To be enlightened by all things is to remove the barrier
between Self and Other."

Dogen Zenji

Many New Thoughts Will Be Coming Up
Many New Lights Will Be Shining On The Blocks
That Have Been In Your Way

We need to learn not to judge ourselves for whatever we think and whatever comes up. We need to find a way to come to know ourselves gently, without judgment, without displeasure. We need to find a way to examine all that happens within ourselves without fear. We need to look at our discomfort, agitation, restlessness, boredom and insecurities, etc. We need to find a way to look at ourselves and accept ourselves just as we are. Only then will we learn to love ourselves and stop running away.

We Need To Find Our Gentle Witness

Our Gentle Witness

*"Keep the doors locked and we will be secure," says the ego.
Our heart responds, "But I'm not happy like that."
To which the ego replies, "Better safe than sorry."*

Ram Dass and Paul Gorman

Remember the meditation instructions which taught you to watch your thoughts? You also learned to watch your feelings and emotions and not to judge them. We must learn to accept what is before we can change anything.

While meditating, we watch our thoughts come in and pass on, our feelings come up and go away. The more we are detached from our thoughts and feelings, the more we learn that they are not permanent, that they come and they go, that they change. They do not remain the same. As we continue to do our sitting meditation we begin to experience this more and more. We are actually training our minds to continue this process throughout the entire day.

When we begin to watch ourselves, it is as if we have a second person watching our minds work. It is as if we have developed a gentle witness who does not get caught up in our soap operas, who does not become a news commentator, who does not judge us or our thoughts or our actions as right or wrong. This witness becomes like a best friend, someone who is always there and just *is* with us. A friend that notices and points out, but doesn't judge.

With this witness, we can begin to trust ourselves. We begin to see ourselves and learn about ourselves.

It is through practicing like this that we begin to become more gentle with ourselves. We slowly change negative tapes to positive ones, and old habitual ways of doing things to a newer healthier way. As we become more gentle with ourselves, we begin to love ourselves. And as we begin to love ourselves, we become more open and we are able to love others in a more richly satisfying manner.

The Buddha taught that the very basic roots of suffering came from resistance to unpleasant situations. We are either trying to hold on to something very tightly because we are afraid that we are going to lose it or we are trying desperately to get something that we do not have. He saw that we would always have pain in our lives but that was not our enemy. Our biggest enemy was our resistance to it.

As addicts and co-dependents we have resisted and hidden from pain all our lives. Not only have we run from pain, but from discomfort, fear, unpleasantness, restlessness, boredom, etc. We never learned how to deal with any of this suffering except by running away. And if we didn't put something into our bodies to block our feelings, or looked for another person or place to make it better, our minds would fantasize and rationalize so that we did not have to hear and face the truth.

As we blocked the feelings that we didn't want to deal with, we blocked the truth. *We closed our hearts.* We also locked the door on love.

> **"I will be my own best friend today and treat myself gently, with love and respect."**

We Now Move To The Next Step Of Our Path.

1. We quiet our minds through meditation.
2. We begin to gain insight into our minds.
3. We begin to accept so that we can change.

Personal Prescription
For Second Week

1. Begin to increase meditation to 20 minutes in the morning and the evening. Begin to listen more to the thoughts and feelings that come up for you that take you away from your breath and begin to let them become your meditation.

2. Continue to bring your full attention to one activity that you do daily, such as brushing your teeth or taking a shower. Continue to notice yourself and everything that goes on for you during this time, including everything that takes your attention away and your reactions.

3. Begin to notice your self-talk. Begin to listen to what the voice in your head is telling you. Keep a record of your self-talk. Remember not to judge anything that comes up, positive or negative. Just bring awareness . . . gentle awareness as you begin to discover the blocks that are on your path.

4. Have a beautiful

   and peaceful

   week full of insight and learning

   . . . Be gentle with yourself

   Keep it simple . . . simple . . . simple.

Commitment

I will meditate for a minimum of 10 minutes at least one, but preferably two, times a day.

I will bring my full attention to the following habit or routine that I do daily ―――――――――――――――.

I will gently bring attention to my self-talk.

Observations

I have made the following new discoveries as a result of this commitment:

It can be helpful to cut this out and paste it up on a file card to carry around with you as a reminder.

---

1. Today I will meditate at least 10 to 20 minutes.
2. I will bring my full attention to one daily activity and stay with it as fully as possible, learning to be in the *now* . . . in the *moment*.
3. I will not *judge* but just accept what I hear and learn from it.
4. I will begin to *listen* to my self-talk and write down the negative tapes that I discover.

Second Week Checklist

	Mon	Tues	Wed	Thur	Fri	Sat	Sun
Morning Meditation							
Morning Inspirational Readings							
Visualizations							
Morning Affirmations							
Bringing Attention to My Self-talk							
Bringing Attention To One Routine							
Evening Inspirational Readings							
Evening Meditation							
Visualizations							
Evening Affirmations							

If it ever becomes difficult to follow this .program on a daily basis, read the section on "When It Is Hard to Meditate". You will see it is not only you. Use the affirmations provided so that you will look forward to it, rather than find it a chore. But if you find it difficult, let those feelings and thoughts be your meditation and notice how you handle such situations. Use it as a learning experience.

Week 3

Personal Plan For Meditation Plus

"The longest journey is the journey inward, for he who has chosen his destiny has started upon his quest for the source of his being."
Dag Hammarsjkold

We are now moving into an exciting segment where you will learn how you are in charge of your life and your experiences.

Writing Third Week's Experiences

Date _____

Reflect on the importance of this week before moving on. Remember that what you learn in your sitting meditation is insight to take with you in all the rest of your life activities. For example, if you become restless in meditation, how do you respond? What are your feelings? Thoughts? Do you want to quit? How is this the same when you are restless in a job or a relationship, in a line or in traffic? Do you get upset or angry? What are the feelings that come up for you? How did you want to respond? Do you quit?

As you begin more and more to watch without judgment, learning will begin to happen for you more rapidly.

1. How did I respond to the variety of feelings that came up during meditation this week?

2. How did I feel different this week?

3. When I brought my attention to one routine, I . . .

4. When I brought up my attention to my self-talk, I discovered . . .

5. I accomplished more _____ less _____ same _____ this week.

6. I learned these new things about me . . .

7. I felt better _____ worse _____ same _____ about myself.

8. I have discovered some new negative tapes that have been blocking my progress . . .

9. Important points to remember . . .

Now go on with your own questions . . . exploring . . . thinking . . . re-feeling.

Pause For Reflections

Date _____

Negative Tapes

"The truth will set you free!"

The further you travel along your path to recovery, the more you will be able to hear the negative tapes that have kept you from reaching your fullest potential. You are now seeing the stumbling blocks that have been your barriers to honest relationships, love and serenity. But most important, you are discovering what has covered your true inner feelings and has kept you from hearing your inner voice and thus connecting with God's will for you.

From the moment of birth we store all the messages that we receive. These messages come from words, touches, feelings, sensations and thoughts. They also come from our perspective of what is happening to us and around us.

You Act Out Who You Think You Are

Imagine your mind like a vast computer, a massive storage depot for all your memories and experiences. Every time you were told you were good and that you were loved, a positive button was pushed. Each time you had a negative experience or message, a negative button was pushed. These messages make up who you *think* you are. Notice the word *think*. You continue to repeat these same messages until you learn or experience different ones.

Each time you are in a new experience which reminds you of an old experience, the old buttons are pushed and you again act as you did in the past. You respond. You react. And your reactions often have little validity or relevance to what is happening today.

Put more simply, the past is stored in your subconscious automatically. In a similar experience, therefore, your subconscious responds and your conscious mind is fooled into thinking that the past is now.

Imagine that there are billions of cells in the brain that are part of circuits that haven't been connected. They have to be wired. Every time we experience something new, wiring is put into place and we have to learn this particular piece of knowledge. There is now a "new mentally created circuit or pathway".

These mental wires make up the network for what we know as our memories, and memories may intrude in disturbing and uninvited ways into our lives. When we experience something new, our brain remembers an old time. Our bodies do not know that it is an old time because the brain is experiencing it now.

We quiet our minds through meditation.

We begin to hear our self-talk.

We begin to see our negative tapes.

We get in touch with the blocks that have been keeping us stuck.

Wish List

Beginning To Turn "It" Around

This is an excellent exercise for shining light on your negative tapes. Spend a few minutes with it. The result can be a turning point in your recovery.

Gently close your eyes for a few moments.

Relax and be comfortable.

Let your relaxation symbol bring relaxation to your mind and your entire body.

Bring yourself to your special sanctuary, your special place. Go to your special place where you are safe and happy, where nothing can harm you in any way.

Let yourself feel what it is like to be there.

Feel the warmth.

Feel the safety.

Feel the comfort.

Feel the happiness.

Take some time to just be there.

Now that you know that you are safe and relaxed in your special place, bring to your mind an image of something you would like to be. This could be anything, such as being in a career, a relationship or an experience. Whatever comes up for you first. It could be your wish to look different or to act different or to be different.

Now picture a new person being exactly how you would like to be. Picture this new person doing whatever it is that you would like to do. Picture how it would feel to be doing it. Imagine how it would feel.

Be that person . . .

Be that person now . . . .

In your mind.

Stay with that person and be that person for a while.

Now gradually come back to the room, and bring this image of the person you would like to be with you. Be here now with your eyes opening, gradually becoming aware of your body in this room with your special image.

Now take your paper, and on one side please write down what it was you imagined. Stay with that image for a while and write down all you can think of that was with you in your mind.

Now turn the paper over and write down all the thoughts that come up for you as to why you can't become that special image.

Examining Our Blocks

You have:

1. Thought about what you wanted to do.
2. Found the reasons that you tell yourself you can't.

3. Learned that these were old negative tapes to which you could choose not to listen. But what's next?

Since we have often been programmed in our past at a subconscious level to feel badly about ourselves, to feel unworthy, we will need to change at two levels. First, we need to see what our defects actually are, and we will go into that in more depth later in this process.

But for a start we can begin to become aware of our negative tapes, through exercises like these, and by just bringing awareness to our everyday lives through sitting and walking meditation, bringing awareness to our *now*.

By shining the light on our *now*, we will see, we will hear, we will feel, we will notice. And once we begin this process, we can never be the same again.

Positive New Image

Who I Would Like To Be

Reasons That Block Me From Achieving That Goal

The Power Of Visualization

"The greatest discovery of any generation is that human beings can alter their lives by altering their attitudes of mind."

— *Albert Schweitzer*

Meditation quiets our minds so we can
see who we are.

Once we see who we are, we have to accept
who we are.

Once we accept who we are, we can eliminate that
which is negative and destructive in our paths.

By emptying ourselves of the negative, we make space
to be filled with the positive.

Once we have become empty, we need to give ourselves new messages so that we can act in new ways. Once the old tapes are gone, visualization is an excellent tool with which to reprogram the computers in our minds. Visualization give our bodies new messages. Our bodies believe what our minds imagine.

Begin A List For Change

As you begin to listen to your self-talk and hear what blocks you from becoming the person you would like to be, start writing it down. Examine your list and pull out one particular block that is standing in your way of doing something you would like to do now.

An example of this could be fear of a job interview. Let us say, for example, that you have an appointment next week. Every time you think about this event your stomach turns, your hands begin to get sweaty and your mind goes blank. You try to think about what you are going to say and nothing comes.

Most likely old images from other times come into your mind. Other times that you have had poor interviews might be there for you. Or times when old tapes played that you weren't as good as other people. How about the time that you were called on in school and you forgot all the answers and felt foolish in front of the entire class. These were the tapes that you got in touch with as you listened to your self-talk.

Now put yourself into a relaxed state.

Bring up your relaxation symbol.

Gradually begin to quiet your mind and begin to picture yourself getting ready for a very successful interview. Picture yourself dressed very appropriately so that you feel very good about yourself. Take a look in the mirror of your mind and know that you look terrific!

Now let yourself be filled with powerful, positive feelings.

Feel yourself confident.

Fill yourself with confidence and good feelings.

Know you are perfect for this job.

Know that there is not a better person than you for this job.

Now let yourself see yourself going though all the scenes of the interview. Picture yourself sitting down in a chair in the office. See the person who is interviewing you sitting in a chair across from you. Know that no matter what this person looks like, there is real concern and caring about you and your ability to do the job. Carry on an imaginary conversation. When you are through, thank this person very much and leave the office.

Absolutely know that if this job is right for you, you will get it. If it is not, the right job is going to appear very quickly.

Let yourself feel the good feelings of having had a successful interview. Let yourself know that you have done a good job.

Congratulate yourself!

After doing this visualization for a few days, your thoughts will begin to change about the upcoming interview and you will actually begin to feel more relaxed and confident about it. By the time that the interview really takes place, you will be able to walk in as if you have been there before, and you will not experience the panic that you might have had in a brand new situation.

Visualizations work because the mind gives the body positive messages. Your body begins to be used to experiencing new ways to feel. New tapes are created and new buttons are pushed.

Whenever you are doing something new, learn to visualize it first in a positive way. Always see yourself as the person you would like to be, acting in a way that you would like to act. *Never* allow old visions to come in from the past. Each time you play back an old unsuccessful picture, your body will act as if it is happening today. Every time you allow yourself to replay an old negative tape, your body will respond as if it is being said to you today. You will reinforce the unsuccessful, negative unhappy picture of yourself and make it harder and harder to change.

> *Visualizations work by themselves but they work more effectively and with more ease and flow when they are combined with affirmations.*

letting go of old negative
self-talk (tapes) and
filling in the space with
peace, love and goodness!

Affirmations

A Tool To Turn Stumbling Blocks Into Ste þ þ þ ing Stones

Affirmations are wonderful tools to help us turn around negative thoughts and habits into positive ones. They help us put positive energy into our lives and release the blocks that are holding us back.

The dictionary states that to affirm is to state positively or with confidence; declare to be true. An affirmation is asserting that a fact is so.

If we believe that we are going to change . . .
we are going to change.

An affirmation is a positive thought that we imagine as if it were true in the now. If we say it and feel it with conviction, it will become true. An affirmation is written or stated positively.

Affirming is not the same as wishing and is far more powerful. Affirming states that something is so. It makes firm a statement or a thought. Wishing is a 'maybe it will and maybe it won't'.

Affirmations should always feel right for you. You are not trying to redo something from the past but to create something brand new. They should create a feeling of belief. You should say them with conviction.

Affirmations are positive statements we say to ourselves. They need to have four qualities to be successful.

1. Conviction

If we say them with conviction we begin the process of internalizing the positive statements that we tell ourselves. If we feel what we tell ourselves is true in the present, our affirmation does become true in the present.

If you really do not believe what you are affirming but you sincerely want it to be true, then give it "lip service". Act as if you believe it. If you "act as if" enough times, you will come to believe it to be true.

As you say it with conviction, you are *energizing* your affirmation. Let yourself *feel* your affirmation by actually visualizing it as real in the now. Let the good *feelings* pour through your body as you begin to reprogram yourself.

2. Present Tense

We state them as if they are happening and real now. We do not say this will happen because that is denying its existence in the now. By telling ourselves it is now real, it will become real in our subconscious. The subconscious does not know if something is happening in reality or only in the mind. It registers feelings and emotions. Therefore, if it is real in the mind, it is real in the subconscious.

3. Energy

Affirmations must be said with positive feelings and with energy. They have to be stated so that they are felt with your body. For example, if you are affirming that you feel good about yourself, imagine how your body would feel if you felt good and became aware of those bodily feelings.

4. Repetition

Affirmations must be repeated either orally or in writing for them to become part of us. Experiments have proved that we can change in 21 days if we repeat our affirmations at least 10 times each day.

love

peace   joy

"I am hearing these messages and I am okay!"

To state something positive about ourselves is probably a very unfamiliar point of view for many of us who have been so used to thinking of ourselves in a negative fashion.

Very often we automatically react to anything good we want to do or think we want to be by saying "I can't" or "I don't deserve." And then we give ourselves a lot of stories and rationalizations to make "I can't" seem real. These negative tapes (thoughts) are the *blocks* that keep us from finding our true self, from finding the good within us.

These are old tapes from yesterday. This is how we let our yesterdays control our todays and this is why things do not change and get better.

By giving up alcohol, drugs and other dependencies, we have made a very powerful positive statement. We have removed the biggest blocks we had. We made extraordinary miraculous progress. We have probably acted on the first bit of faith in positives in a long time. Things surely don't feel better when we withdraw and deprive ourselves of something we so desperately want. But we begin to believe that if we stay away from these substitutes for long enough, our lives will be better. Now, in abstinence we come in touch with the insanity of our minds, especially when our minds tell us that just one drink or drug or sweet or whatever will make us feel better.

And the longer that we stay away from the things we are addicted to, add a recovery program to our lives and then begin to meditate, the more we begin to hear all the other negative and destructive tapes that have kept us in places that are not good for us and kept us filled with feelings that we do not want to have.

The important things to remember about affirmations are that . . .

1. *They are stated in the present tense, in the* NOW.
2. *They are positive.*
3. *You act and feel as if they are true.*
4. *You feel good about what you are saying.*
5. *You repeat them at least 10 times a day for 21 days.*

"God is giving me all the energy that I need to make positive changes in my life today!"

It is time to get unblocked.

It is time to be rid of those blocks that have kept us
imprisoned in our past for so long.

Here are a few examples of affirmations:

I am discovering who I am with joy.

*Today I feel the Power and the Energy of the universe
at my fingertips.*

I am moving through this day easily and effortlessly.

I deserve wonderful things to happen to me.

I am finding a life for me that is perfect for who I am.

*I have all the time that I need to do all that is good and
right in my life.*

I am a lovable and loving person.

My Higher Power is always with me and guiding me.

I am connected with the positive and loving energies of the universe.

Now write your affirmation 10 times. As you write it, you are SEEing it on paper. As you write it you are SAYing it to yourself in your mind and creating a new SELF-TALK. Then say it out loud so that you can HEAR it. As you say it, say it with feelings so that you can energize your body. You are using all your senses to make a new impression, a new positive tape.

1

2

3

4

5

6

7

8

9

10

Personal Prescription for Third Week

1. Continue to increase meditation to minimum of 20 minutes morning and evening and to listen to the thoughts and feelings that come up for you that take you away from your breath. Begin to let them become your meditation.
2. Continue to get to know your self-talk. Find a name for that self-talk voice that has made a home in your head for so many years. Begin to gradually learn how to reduce his or her power over you.
3. Continue to bring your full attention to one activity that you do daily such as brushing your teeth or taking a shower. Continue to notice yourself and everything that goes on for you during this time, including everything that takes your attention away and your reactions to it.
4. *Visualize* a new goal. Begin to see yourself in a new, positive way in your mind.
5. Write your affirmations that affirm the new picture you have of yourself to change your negative tapes to positive tapes.
6. Bring yourself thoughts of love.

Know that you deserve to be happy . . .

You deserve to be peaceful . . .

You deserve to be free from suffering.

"God is giving me all the energy that i need to make positive changes in my life today"

Commitment

I will meditate a minimum of 20 minutes at least one, but preferably two, times a day.

I will bring my full attention to the following habit or routine that I do daily _____.

I will begin my new visualizations and affirmations.

Observations

I have made the following new discoveries as a result of this commitment:

Third Week Checklist

	Mon	Tues	Wed	Thur	Fri	Sat	Sun
Morning Meditation							
Morning Inspirational Readings							
Visualizations							
Morning Affirmations							
Bringing Attention to My Self-talk							
Bringing Attention to One Routine							
Evening Inspirational Readings							
Evening Meditation							
Visualizations							
Evening Affirmations							

Week 4

Personal Plan
For Meditation Plus

By now meditation is becoming as close to being a daily habit as brushing your teeth if you have been doing it on a regular basis. And you have probably discovered the value of bringing your full attention to your breath helpful in other stress areas of your life as well. When you find yourself angry or negative or uptight anywhere, any-time . . . just bring your full attention to your breathing and experience the release.

As you are able to quiet yourself down more regularly and make more space to be in the *now*, you should be experiencing more feelings of love and compassion at the most unexpected moments. These fringe benefits will include bringing you closer and closer to others. You will see more and more of the similarities and less of the differences between you and the other people in the world.

If this is not the case with you, and you are still having difficulty meditating on a regular basis, know that you are not alone. In this section we will cover many helpful tools that will improve your discipline *if you want to*.

feel the goodness

Writing Fourth Week's Experiences

Date _____

1. How did I respond to the variety of feelings that came up during meditation this week?

2. How did I feel different this week?

3. When I brought my attention to one routine, I . . .

4. When I brought my attention to myself as a *listener*, I discovered . . .

5. I accomplished more _____ less _____ same _____ this week.

6. I learned these new things about me . . .

7. I felt better _____ worse _____ same _____ about myself.

8. Important points to remember:

Pause For Reflections

Date _____

I'm Having A Hard Time

Meditate even when your self-talk says . . .

"I don't want to meditate"

or

"I don't have time to meditate"

or

"Meditating isn't working"

or

etc.

etc.

etc.

. . . or even,

**"I don't know what's wrong with me but
I just can't seem to meditate."**

Over and over again I hear these words from people who have at one time or other meditated with great results. I have struggled to figure out how to help them, how to make it easier for them. I have finally concluded that I can't really do that. That they (and you, if and when you find yourself in this position) must find a way to bring discipline into your life and meditate even when you don't want to do so.

Why is it that we don't always do what is best for us? Why do we put off completing things that we know we will feel good about when we are finished? Perhaps it is as simple as procrastination or laziness. Perhaps we just want what we want when we want it and we would rather be doing something else at the time. Maybe it doesn't give us immediate gratification and we think that sleeping an extra 20 minutes would "feel better".

Rather than even trying to figure it out, bring logic to it or to psychoanalyze it, let's keep it really simple. Let's just say that it comes from a negative system that we don't want in our lives anymore. And with all that we have learned so far about changing our negative thought system by meditating, visualizing, acting "as if" and stopping our negative self-talk, just know that with a simple painless and gentle plan, you can get back on the positive Path to Recovery and meditate without pain and struggle again.

Feels As If You Are On A Detour?

If you can identify with this dilemma, know that just a few extra minutes of gentleness are needed. Don't beat yourself or judge yourself. Know that it is quite common, that most of us have been there at some time or other. If you use this as an opportunity to watch yourself and get to know yourself better in this kind of situation, great progress can be made. Use it as a stepping stone and not a stumbling block.

Know that all you need is a willingness, or as we have said before, even a willingness to be willing. Here are a few suggestions that you can use to make this journey back easier.

Watch Yourself "Not Want To Meditate" Just As You Watch A Thought In Meditation

When the thought comes up that "I don't want to . . ." or "I can't" or "There is no time" or whatever, watch the thoughts as you would a cloud going by in the sky. As you gently watch the thoughts without judging them, they become lighter and lighter until they pass by and disappear.

Watch them . . . just notice them and say "Oh, there I am again in this place. It's OK to be in this place."

Begin with a few affirmations to put you in the right frame of mind. Here are some suggested ones. Add others that will work for you.

"Today I am beginning my Spiritual Path to recovery."

"Nothing can stop me from growing today!"

"Today I am willing to meditate . . . whether I feel like it or not!"

"I'm Having A Hard Time" Visualization

Here is a visualization that will help you be fully awake, earlier in the morning. Do this right before going to bed so that it will be working on your subconscious while you are sleeping. You will not have to do anything at all but picture the scene and repeat the affirmations afterward.

Go very gently into your special place, your inner sanctuary. Find a wall or a flat surface and create a very beautiful clock. Design this clock out of any material you wish, with a special decoration just for you. Set the hands of the clock for twenty minutes earlier than you usually get up. Know that when you get up twenty minutes earlier tomorrow morning, you will do this without feeling deprivation. You will not be tired at all. In fact, you will wake up refreshed and looking forward to meditating.

"I'm Having A Hard Time" Affirmation

Affirmations that have worked for others with this difficulty:

"I am looking forward to meditating in the morning!"

"God is giving me all the strength and direction that I need to meditate regularly."

"I meditate with joy and peace."

Take Five

Meditations
For When You Who Think
You Have No Time To Meditate

For the days when you are racing, with both your head and with your body, take just five minutes to read this meditation. When you are going full steam ahead and wonder why you are always busy, when you haven't one moment for yourself and wonder how you will ever be through with your list of things you "must" do; when you wonder if you will ever have time to stop with friends or smell a rose, take five minutes to experience miracles!

Repeat the following words . . . slowly . . . taking at least five minutes to finish this exercise. Notice the changes occurring in you physically and mentally while you are reading this. (This particular meditation works even better if you can stop long enough to find someone to read it to you!)

- •
- •
- •

Now just close your eyes for a few minutes and picture a clock. Design this clock out of any material you wish, with a special decoration just for you. Set the hands of the clock for five minutes from now. Know that you have enough time to take five minutes and feel good about yourself for doing it. Now open your eyes if you are doing this alone and read the following slowly, or just listen carefully if it is being read to you . . .

I have all the time that I need in the

universe

today.

I have all the time and the energy that I need

today.

I have all the time and the energy and the

direction that I need

today.

to do all that God wants me to do with my

life

today.

My struggling is over.

I have turned over all my rushing to my Higher

Power and it is out of my hands

today.

I am very slowly and

   very gently

      going to go on with my day,

grateful that a Power greater than myself

   is supplying me with all that I need

      to do all that is good and right in my

         life . . .

           today.

                  Thank You!

" . . . my struggle is over.
i have turned over all my
rushing to my Higher Power.

When Meditation Isn't Going Well

Sometimes we suddenly seem to come to a dead stop in our progress. We might think we are doing everything the same, but something is changing. This is usually a place for new answers. A time for patience.

It is then that we are judging ourselves too much. Be soft and loving and remember your *Gentle Witness*. If there is turmoil, remember that there is a reason. There is something to learn. Peace is not always possible. It is impossible to have something different than we have right now.

There are times when we have to go through layers and layers of insights to find the answer. Only by going through our struggles and by sharing them with others so that they can see our victory over them by the power of God in our lives . . . do we become a light for others to follow.

Sometimes we need to try softer.

"Even in moments of doubt I know my Higher Power is guiding me on my path today."

" there are times when we have to go through layers and layers of insight to find the answer."

Finding Our Inner Guide

*"As we open the connections between the conscious and the
subconscious aspects of our beings, we reclaim our
spiritual selves from isolation and neurosis."*

WomanSpirit

You are now in the process of removing the negative, destructive
messages that have been holding you back and keeping you stuck. You
are beginning to see that you have created these tapes. They really
originated from others in your early life, and you have taken them on
as your own by accepting them as truth and recording them in your
subconscious. The more you meditate, the more this new awareness
deepens.

As you go farther into your reprogramming process and begin to
change negative tapes to positive ones, where are you going to receive
your answers? Who will give you your truth? If your past tapes no
longer work for you, where do you go from here?

*"you have buried your inner goddess
and it is time to set her free!"*

Deep within all of us lives our own truth at a level that we have rarely been able to trust consistently. Now that you know that you have a special place within you where you can always go and feel safe and find peace, special answers will soon be yours.

Deep within you, at that very special place where your spark of life is beginning to twinkle and shine again, lies your inner knowledge at a very basic level. Call it intuition . . . inner knowing . . . natural knowing. Whatever you want to call it, it is yours and you are the only one who can find it.

Inside your special place lives an Inner Guide, who can be called your Inner God or Goddess, a Special Friend, a Sponsor or any other name that makes you feel comfortable. I call mine my Inner Goddess. For the sake of ease I will refer to her as an Inner Goddess from now on. You can just substitute your own name whenever you choose.

Your Inner Goddess has always been there. You just covered her up every time you were hurt and disappointed. Every time you had an unpleasant experience you covered her with layer after layer of blocks. Each time you saw your parents fighting . . . each time you were abused or attacked or put down or abandoned . . . you put on another layer. You became less and less able to feel your emotions and less and less able to trust yourself. Every time you turned to a drink or a drug or another dependency or escape, she hid deeper within you and further away from your reach.

removing
negatives tapes!

inside your special place
lives an inner guide.

You have buried your Inner Goddess and it is time to set her free! It is time to give rebirth to sleeping parts of yourself long buried in fear, guilt, frozen anger, resentments, memories, alcohol, drugs and other dependencies. It's time to find your own truth.

Special Meditation To Find Your Inner Guide

Let yourself relax. Begin to get ready to go to your special place inside . . . your inner sanctuary, so that you can meet your inner guide.

Take all the time you need to be comfortable. Let yourself feel your relaxation symbol. Begin to bring your full attention to your breath. Let your mind slowly settle down and be quiet.

Quietly

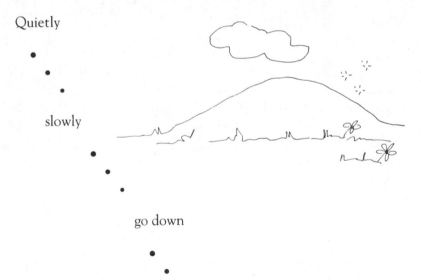

slowly

go down

to your special place.

Bring in good feelings about yourself.

Let yourself know that you are safe and that this is a place where only good can happen. Let your entire body feel at peace.

Now let yourself be out of doors. Take time to look around and feel what the weather is with your entire body. Look up at the sky and see if it is clear or cloudy. Maybe there are just a few clouds that are drifting by. Feel the time of day and the time of year. Do you hear any birds or animals. Is there a special scent of grass or flowers? Feel the ground beneath your feet. Bend down and touch the earth with your fingers. Pick up some dirt and let it run through your fingers and fall back to the ground. Hear the sound as it hits the ground.

Look up and see a winding path before you. The path goes as far as your eye can see and ends at the top of a hill. Know that someone is walking slowly toward you on the other side of the hill. Very gradually a head is beginning to appear and then an entire body. Begin to walk toward that person. See if you can see what she* is wearing and what she looks like. Can you make out the features on her face?

When you are close enough, reach out your hand in welcome. Walk slowly back with her to your special place. Be welcoming and thank her for coming to you. Ask her for a name. Tell her yours.

When you get inside your special place, take time to show her around and make her comfortable. Sit across from her and look directly into her eyes. Ask her if she has a special message for you.

Share where you are in your life and tell her about a problem you are now having. Ask her if she has any advice or answers for you.

If you don't hear any answers, do not be concerned. This will come in time. Just sit there quietly. Be with each other. It is fine if you do not hear words or even if you don't see her. Just know that she is there. In time all this will become clearer and clearer.

Whenever you feel ready, say goodbye and thank her for being there.

Know that you can bring her back any time you want. Know that you can share anything with her and it will be safe. You can trust her completely.

Stay with your good feelings for a while.

Get ready to bring these good feeling of trust back with you.

Know that you never have to be alone again.

Very gradually get ready to come back to your room. Be sure you count to five before you open your eyes.

(*I have used the word "she" or "her" for convenience. Use whatever pronoun that you want for your inner guide.)

Expanding Our Comfort Zone

When we are used to doing things in the same way, there is a sense of comfort. Even if this way is not positive or healthy for us, we are still comfortable in it. We are used to it. We know what to expect from it, even if we are not happy with the results. It's like wearing an old robe that is torn and tattered but oh so comfortable.

If we make drastic changes, anxiety is often the result. Not only is it difficult to do things in a new way, but it is also very frightening. We leave our comfort zone and begin to experience panic.

leaving your comfort zone...
out to make new + tapes!

If we make small changes, take small risks, we can handle them without too much anxiety. But if the changes are big, all the feelings of anxiety and fear set in and we want to run back to our comfort zone quickly. And most often the old thoughts of escape come in again and we want to go back to blocking those unpleasant feelings. Destructive thoughts return to our addiction and dependencies.

It can also sometimes be frightening to be going along a new path and not know what is before you. Faith is something that develops, a day at a time, by an experience at a time. But knowing that everything is going to be all right in our head does not necessarily immediately convey that message to our bodies. That takes time. Changing old tapes takes time.

By using our visualizations to see ourselves in a new scene over and over again, we create new imprints in our minds and bodies until we feel as if the new picture is real. When we are ready to make the change, we will have already lived the scene in our minds and therefore we will not experience the panic that we would have if we suddenly made a drastic change.

After we visualize ourselves in this new picture, feeling it fully with all our senses, affirmations firm up our new picture even further.

What Do I Want?

You must first have a clear picture of what you want before you can expect to change and grow. Confusion and conflict come when you are not sure, and your imagination wars with your subconscious and you cannot decide between two or three choices.

> "Though the wide universe is full of good, no kernel of nourishing corn can come to him but through his toil bestowed on the plot of ground which is given to him to till. The power which resides in him is new in nature, and none but he knows what that is which he can do, nor does he know until he has tried."
>
> Emerson

If your picture is not clear, spend some time here recording your thoughts. Write about your confusion and meditate on it. It often helps to do a meditation and visualization with your inner guide and ask the questions that you cannot answer. Then let it go. Give up the struggle and trust that the answers will come. They will.

"there are times when we have to go through layers and layers of insight to find the answer."

Meditation For Clearing Or Unblocking

Use your relaxation symbol and meditate for at least five minutes before entering into this visualization.

Spend a few minutes in your special place, knowing that your inner guide is always there to lead you to truth and peace and safety.

Now move outside your special place and wander down a winding path toward a wide river.

Feel the breeze as it brushes against your face and skin, blowing in your hair. Let the sun beat on your face for a few minutes as you listen to the sound of the water as it is flowing from the hill above down to a wall or dam. Find yourself wandering to that side.

There is a log floating in the water coming toward you. Climb on the log and let it carry you through the water. See how twigs and leaves and trash have built up on this side of the wall and can't get through.

You can barely see to the other side of the water. Let the log float over to the wall and climb up on the wall and look over to the other side. Notice how the water is calm and clear and beautiful, and flowers grow on the sides of the shore.

See how muddy your side is with all the debris churning and floating around. See that the wall is nothing more than a pile of all this debris that has clung together, holding the water back, not letting it flow free and clear.

Take the wall down piece by piece and let them float to the shore. Now watch the water as it flows to the clearer side, joining the rest of the stream now, flowing freely. In the same way, see that each of your own blocks is a character defect or an obsession or negative trait that is holding you back from letting your energy flow freely and positively.

See what has been holding you back and look at what you are willing to let go of.

Let yourself feel the freedom of your wall coming down. Feel your energy flowing freely as your load becomes lighter and lighter, no longer carrying the burdens of yesterday.

See your reflection in the clear waters and smile at yourself as you know that you are now creating more space for positive energy to come into your life.

Now slowly go back to your special place and rest awhile, knowing that you will soon return to this room energized and renewed and healed.

"Pain comes from not wanting to let go of a position that has helped us get to where we are."

Ruth Ross

1. List everything in your life that you really don't want anymore (ie, confusion, clutter, anger or, more specifically, an unhappy job or tight money conditions, negative relationship).

" i visualize myself as if this has already occurred ! "

2. List everything that you would like to have (ie, clarity, order, peace, a different job, abundant money, a healthy relationship).

3. Now choose ONE of the things you would like to have out of your life today and decide to no longer have it.

   Today I am positively letting go of . . .

   I visualize myself as if this has already occurred . . .

   My affirmation for this expectancy is . . .

   Goal date . . .

4. Now choose *one* of the things you would like to have in your life today and make the intention to have it.

   Today I have a positive expectancy of . . .

   I visualize myself as if this has already occurred . . .

   My affirmation for this expectancy is . . .

   Goal date . . .

Remember: You must empty before you can fill. As you are willing to let go of the people, places and things that are destructive or negative in your life today, you will become open to positive changes and additions to take place.

Wish List: 21-Day Exercise

Use the wish list exercise from an earlier week. Picture yourself already in a situation that you would like to be in. Feel how good it would feel.

" . . . you must empty before you can fill."

Then let all the reasons that you can't have this wish come up for you. Write down all these reasons.

Now let yourself see these reasons as excuses. See them as blocks that you have always used to tell yourself why you can't have what you want or would like to have. Accept them as more of your negative tapes.

Now use your affirmations to change these tapes into positive messages!

Affirmations

Personal Prescription for Fourth Week

Continue to meditate at least 20 minutes morning and evening and continue to listen to the thoughts and feelings that come up for you that take you away from your breath. Let them be your meditation until they disappear and then go back to your breathing.

Continue to be aware of your self-talk. Just notice it, accept it and move back to your breath.

In the second week's homework, you listened to yourself talk. Now notice how you *listen* to others. Get in touch with your feelings and thoughts as you *hear* others speak. Notice yourself as a *listener*.

Continue to bring your full attention to one activity that you do daily, such as brushing your teeth or taking a shower. Continue to notice yourself and everything that goes on for you during this time, including everything that takes your attention away and your reactions to it.

And don't forget your affirmations. They will open new doors on your path.

letting go of old excuses (blocks)

Commitment

Date _____

I will meditate a minimum of 20 minutes at least one, but preferably two, times a day.

I will bring my full attention to the following habit or routine that I do daily _____.

Observations

I have made the following new discoveries as a result of this commitment:

Fourth Week Checklist

	Mon	Tues	Wed	Thur	Fri	Sat	Sun
Morning Meditation							
Morning Inspirational Readings							
Visualizations							
Morning Affirmations							
Bringing Attention to My Self-talk							
Bringing Attention to One Routine							
Evening Inspirational Readings							
Evening Meditation							
Visualizations							
Evening Affirmations							

Week 5

Personal Plan for Meditation Plus

This week we will delve further into the blocks that keep us from being the best of who we are. We will learn more about that special safe place inside where we find our truth. It will become easier to trust ourselves and our own instincts. This is an exciting week because many blocks will fall away and your path will become wider and wider as more possibilities open in your life.

Remember, this is your journey. So do whatever you are ready to do. No more. No less.

Writing Fifth Week's Experiences

1. How did I respond to the variety of feelings that came up during meditation this week?

2. How did I feel different this week?

3. When I brought my attention to one routine, I . . .

4. When I brought my attention to myself as a talker, I discovered . . .

5. I accomplished more _____ less _____ same _____ this week.

6. I learned these new things about me . . .

7. I felt better _____ worse _____ same _____ about myself.

8. I have found new positive things about me . . .

Now go on with your own questions . . . exploring . . . thinking . . . re-feeling.

Pause For Reflections

Date _____

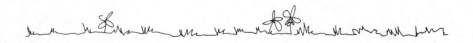

What Are Our Blocks?

Imagine that you have been on a very long journey. In fact, you have. You have traveled your entire life to get to this very moment. As you have been learning, each experience and feeling that you have had has been recorded on a computer disk. By now you will have built up quite a collection of computer disks, each one full of memories.

Our minds are very much like computers. We have a conscious and subconscious mind. We use our conscious mind approximately 10% of the time while our subconscious mind is controlling us 90% of the time.

Some of these messages take the form of guilt and shame. Others come masked as a poor self-image. And yet others stay around as fear and resentments and anger, to mention only a few.

Every experience that we have had is recorded in our subconscious. It just stays there, recorded. It does not do anything until it is called upon. Every thought that we have had is recorded in our subconscious, too.

Our subconscious does not know the difference between real and imagined experiences. If you had been slapped as a child, that experience, the visual picture and the feelings that took place at the time of that experience are recorded. If the same person threatened you again with punishment, and every time you saw that person you relived the feelings of the first beating, your subconscious would record those feelings as if they had happened again, reinforcing your fear of that person.

Maybe you attended school on a day when you were not prepared to be called on and, of course, were called on. The embarrassment of not knowing the answer created terrible feelings of stress, anxiety and guilt. Often the stress you felt was so great that the next time that you were called upon, you relived that incident in your subconscious mind. Even if you were prepared, memory of the old incident created stress in the new incident. The new stress took over and your mind went blank. You couldn't remember any of the answers.

Now we know that all of us are born with a spark of pure love within, and we have seen how the years of experiences, real and imagined, have covered this spark of energy and love.

We are survivors, however. Anyone who has lived till this moment and is still alive and able to read this page is a survivor. In order to survive we have thought it necessary to protect ourselves from pain and unhappiness. We have done this with our drugs, alcohol and other dependencies and we have done this by building defense mechanisms. We have done what we thought we had to do so that we wouldn't feel that dreadful pain of rejection and disappointment.

continue to reach within for that special spark... continue to grow in inner peace..."

So we have built walls with such self-talk as . . .

"I don't care if I'm not invited."
"I'd rather be alone anyway."
"No one will ever understand me."
"I'll never be smart enough to be successful."
"I have a terrible memory."

As we are becoming more and more aware, we have produced these tapes for ourselves at a subconscious level. Usually we did not even know when we created them. Often they have originated in what someone else said to us such as a parent telling us that we are no good.

We hear what they think of us, their image of us, and we take it on as truth for our own self-image.

If we do not feel as good as everyone else, of course, we would rather stay home from a party. We have experienced embarrassment and rejection in the past and think that if we go to another party, we will just repeat the same unpleasant experience. Of course, we think that we are happier alone.

Along with these pictures of unpleasant memories, we have carried the pain of the unpleasant experience as well. We have continued to feel angry and resentful at some people from our past. We have to be willing to let these go.

List here some of the unpleasant memories
you are still carrying from the past.

Forgiveness

One of the biggest blocks to peace is holding on to anger and resentments and self-pity. Full recovery is impossible without forgiveness. Peace of mind is impossible without forgiveness. A point will come where further growth is impossible without forgiveness.

Lack of forgiveness holds us back and keeps us stuck in misery. Some of the things that we insist on holding on to when we refuse to forgive are . . .

Anger	Fear
Resentments	Guilt
Being Right	Shame
Staying Still	Being a Victim
Dependencies	Hate
Blame	Getting Even

The list could go on and on.

forgiveness ♥

Resentments keep us in the past. We cannot be in the now when we resent. When we resent, we relive the old feelings over and over again. As already explained, our bodies do not know the difference between a real experience and a thought. If you are re-feeling, reliving a past experience in your mind, your body responds as if the act were happening right now. So when you remember something that you are angry about, the feelings of anger replay throughout your body, doing damage to it.

The root of the word forgive is to *let go*.

Even when we know how damaging holding on is, why is it so hard to let go?

Until we know that we benefit from forgiving, we will never want to change. Until we know that we really forgive so that we can feel better, for our own peace of mind, we will continue to hang on to resentments and be miserable.

What we are actually holding on to is only a memory of an event that happened in the past. It is no longer real in the now. It is only a memory that we have in our minds and, therefore, re-feel in our bodies and emotions.

Imagine yourself in a very good frame of mind. Now imagine someone who has made statements that have caused you pain. Let yourself feel your feelings about those statements. Now imagine that this person has just come into your room. This person does not say a word but merely looks at you. You no longer feel good but remember the other times that you have felt pain. Without anything new happening, you have given this person the power to take away all your good feelings.

Another word for forgiveness is *atonement*. **A Course of Miracles** talks about atonement as At-One-Ment or becoming one with the other person. Atonement is a correction of our belief of separation. We become *at one* by becoming willing to give up that which separates us. We become *at one* when we know that we are both children of the universe with the same purpose deep within. We feel at peace when we find our similarities, not our differences.

Forgiveness is a Choice

"How do you know whether to choose the stairs to heaven or the way to hell? Quite easily. How do you feel? Is peace your awareness? Are you certain which way to go? . . . If not, you walk alone."

A Course of Miracles

I sometimes find it very helpful to picture the other peson with a heart inside their body in the shape of a valentine heart. And then I picture a similar heart within me. I can finally overlook the events that have happened that are standing between us. I then can see that the events are only memories in my mind and no longer exist in reality.

you

events between us

"*A cloud does not put out the sun.*"

A Course of Miracles

No matter what we are thinking and feeling, our suffering and resentments do not change the fact that somewhere within the other person, however deeply buried it might be, they, too, have a spark of love and life. Our unwillingness to forgive is all that is standing in the way of our seeing it.

A Course of Miracles teaches that every act is an expression of love or a cry for help. When we know that, we experience a miracle because a miracle is a shift in perception, a change in our awareness. We suddenly see things differently. We experience *at-one-ment*.

The more that we can become empty, the more room we make to be filled.

" ... you must empty before you can fill."

When we become willing to let go of our resentments, we will open up to love. As we are willing to have these blocks removed, letting ourselves be emptied of that which has kept us strangers from our fellow human beings for so long, we will begin to let in love.

As we become filled with love and really begin to experience our sameness, our world will get bigger and bigger. No longer will we be confined within the barriers and limitations of our past need for alikeness. Where we once needed a small circle of friends with same personalities, like race, religious and political beliefs, we now become more and more open to finding love and goodness in everyone.

Forgiveness Exercises

Often we do not know that we still have forgiveness to do. We walk around with uncomfortable feelings and do not know what it is that is standing in the way of our comfort and self-love. These exercises will help you get in touch with old feelings of anger and resentments that might have been buried for years.

Follow the basic meditation instructions that bring you to your special place with your inner guide.

Ask your inner guide to help you find anyone in your past who you need to release.

List everyone here who comes up for you.

Bring each person, one at a time, into your inner space. Have them sit down. Bring in a chair and sit directly across from them. Look directly into their eyes.

Now tell them everything that you are thinking and feeling about them. Tell it *all*. Don't hold anything back. Do not judge anything that you are saying or feeling. It all needs to be said and felt. Remember, you are in a special safe place with your inner guide and there is nothing to fear.

When you are completely finished, let them tell you what is going on for them. Listen to their point of view. Again know that they cannot hurt you in any way.

When you are both complete, both stand up and if you can, hug each other. If this is something that does not feel good for you, that is perfectly fine.

You will feel differently about each meeting and your willingness to forgive will vary. Keep knowing that wherever you are with each person is perfect for this time on your path. Each step of willingness carries you farther along to peace.

> *"He who cannot forgive others breaks the bridge which he himself must pass one day."*
>
> Old Proverb

Forgiveness Affirmations

Everyone who has offended me I forgive. Whatever has made me bitter, resentful, unhappy, I forgive. Within and without, I forgive. Things past, things present, things future, I forgive. This includes myself.

Everyone who I have ever offended forgives me. This includes everything that I have done to anyone that I know about and everything that I have done to anyone that I do not know about or do not remember. This includes everything that I have done to anyone whether I was drunk or high or depressed; it includes any state of mind that I was in.

I forgive me for all the hurt and pain that I have caused myself. This includes all times, whether I was sober or straight. It includes everything at any time in any condition.

"I am now forgiven by everything and everyone of the past and present that needs to forgive me. I am now positively forgiven by everyone."* (*The Dynamic Laws of Healing by Catherine Ponder)

Now write your forgiveness affirmations.

Low Self-Esteem

We Act Out Who We Think We Are

Low self-esteem is another large block that holds us back. As you hear more and more of your self-talk, begin writing down all the tapes you hear from your past. Thoughts, feelings, blocks all come up.

During infancy, when we feel very powerless, we build survival mechanisms. When our needs are not being met, when we are afraid and hurt, we begin to build walls of self-protection and learn modes of behavior in order to get along.

This is the time that our images of our selves begin to develop. This is the time that the messages are formed that we are later to replay and replay at the "push of a button". We often refer to our reactions and say that someone has "pushed our buttons". As we have seen, this is exactly the way it happens. When faced with a confrontation, early emotions long stored in our subconscious come up and we respond as we did to the earliest ones, not to today's event. We are not living in reality but on the fantasies and memories of our past.

We must find a way to detach, not to identify with our self-talk so that we may learn how to change and grow. If we are stuck with our solid views of ourselves, we will be committed to continually act out the way we see ourselves.

> *We act like the persons we see ourselves to be.*
> *We act in accordance with our self-image.*
> *When the opinion changes, the performance follows.*
>
> Lou Tice

With low self-esteem we are going to act as if we are unworthy of good relationships, rewarding jobs, success and happiness. If we think we don't deserve good things to happen to us, we will be sure to see that they don't. We will either not go for something good or we will sabotage anything good that comes along.

Know that we do not do this at a conscious level. As you have learned, we are still acting out old tapes from early childhood and we will continue to do so until we know how to change them.

old tapes can keep us from growing

Father Leo Booth, in his book **Spirituality and Recovery,** says, "If we have a poor opinion of ourselves, if we do not think we are of much value, if we are unable to see any good features in our lives, then it is not surprising we are destroying ourselves."

The images we have of ourselves prepare us for either success or failure. We act out our images and opinions of ourselves that often were created in our early formative years.

All our negative past experiences block us from having energy today. We are stuck. We can't move forward until we become unblocked. But just knowing this isn't enough. Many times we know we are blocked. We may even know why we are blocked. Yet we remain still unable to move forward.

So again, we are going to listen to our self-talk. We are going to hear our negative tapes. And as we listen to the very tapes that keep us in a state of low self-esteem. We are going to *shine a light* on them, *accept* them as *blocks* and *visualize* the new way we want to be and be ready to change.

Recording my self-talk that is blocking my positive self-image negative tapes I hear . . .

Turning negative tapes into positive tapes with new affirmations

letting go of old negative self-talk (tapes) and filling in the space with peace, love and goodness!

N.U.T.S.!

A Fun Way To End Negative Thinking

Negative thinking is so often a part of our minds that we rarely notice anything wrong with it. We just take for granted that it is the way that we are. We let negative tapes perpetuate our negativity such as, perhaps, "I'm too old to change" or "You can't teach an old dog new tricks.".

But now that we have learned to . . .

Meditate — to quiet our minds

Listen — to our *self-talk*

Accept — the truth about ourselves, and

Become willing to change . . .

. . . We can no longer accept our negativity as a way of life. We are ready to be good to ourselves and put all this work into action.

REMEMBER. . .

You can only have one thought in your mind at a time. You are at choice about whether that thought is positive or negative.

The more times that we turn a negative thought into a positive one, the deep grooves of the negative tape will wear out and the positive tape will begin to fill in and take its place. In time positive tapes will begin to become the new habit and we will be giving ourselves new messages and getting positive results.

Are you really ready for change? If so, you are now at the point where it is happening.

Each time you hear your self-talk being a negative barrier to your growth, yell . . .

STOP!

know that positive thoughts are just waiting to fill in!

Picture a large red STOP sign with big, black letters that spell STOP!

And then say to yourself . . .

NUTS!

NUTS stands for Negative and Unpleasant Thought-Stopping. Now it is difficult to picture a STOP sign in your mind and yell STOP at yourself without smiling. But it is even more difficult to say NUTS to yourself without smiling.

So remember this little trick. It works!

Trust Your Instincts

Trust Yourself
Trust Your Truth

As we continue this path we are finding out that we do not need to have other people to make us feel good about ourselves. We can begin to trust our own inner truth, our own inner messages. As we continue to wipe out our old negative tapes, forgiving, becoming free from our past and in charge of our today, we begin to trust ourselves.

1. Today I trust the following things about myself . . .

2. I am hearing these new messages and I am okay . . .

3. I will follow my instincts and follow this new short-term goal . . .

4. I will follow my instincts and follow this long-term goal . . .

Use your visualizations exercises to picture yourself as if your new goals are actually true. Continue to affirm them until they are.

The Story Of The Godbag

The Godbag is a wonderful tool to help you let go of the problems and worries that you carry with you. It is also an excellent tool to help you with people who you resent and have a hard time forgiving. It works with fears, anxieties, projections and decisions. In short, as you will see, it is a wonderful tool for just about anything that you cannot handle alone.

In 1976 Sandra Bierig, my partner, and I started Serenity House, a recovery home for alcoholic women. We barely had enough money for food on the table, let alone enough to pay our bills. We were constantly worrying, hardly sleeping at night, wondering where the next meal was going to come from. The strain was really beginning to show when one day a dear friend, Jane, shared a story with us.

She told us the story of a little old lady in California who was very often in trouble. It seemed that every time she tried to do something her way, it would really turn out badly. But she had a Godbag. And the times that she remembered to write down some problem or other and turn it over to her Higher Power by putting it in the Godbag, everything would work out just fine.

Often this little old lady would put a problem in the Godbag but would get impatient while waiting for results. So she would try to handle it herself, until she saw it going badly again and would put it back in the Godbag again mentally. Lo and behold, the problem always worked out just fine when she did that.

Well, if it worked for a little old lady in California, just maybe it would work for us. So Barbara, one of our first residents, stitched a simple Godbag for us out of some green burlap. (We still have it today.) And we all rushed to write down everything that was worrying us.

Miracles did start happening. Donations started coming in. The Division of Alcoholism gave us our first contract. (We have had one with them ever since.) Food seemed to appear from nowhere and donations of beds and bureaus began to arrive at our front door. But the biggest miracle of all was that women started to get sober. And that was, after all, the purpose of it all.

Just like the little old lady from California, every time we became impatient and took our problems back, the worry would return and things started going badly. But when we let them go, things just seemed to work out miraculously.

Godbags work! Thank God!

Godbag Visualization

As you begin all visualizations, find a comfortable, quiet place and relax. Sit quietly and close your eyes and breathe in and breathe out very slowly. Take a few minutes to notice you breath as your breathe in and you breathe out. Bring your attention to your breath as you breathe in and you breathe out.

Relax all parts of your body, bringing attention to any part that might feel strain or anxiety.

And picture in your mind the most beautiful Godbag for yourself . . .
Any color that you like . . .
Any material that you like.

Create your very own Godbag in your mind,
decorating it in
your own special way . . .
either with paints . . .
or with materials . . .
or with stitching
Or anything else that you can think of to make it your very own.
Know that this is a very special bag, a miraculous bag!

You don't even have to call it a Godbag if you'd rather not. It can be your Higher Power Bag or a Positive Energy Bag or whatever you choose.

Now, in your mind get a pencil and paper. Sit very quietly and write down everything that might come up for you that is concerning you right now . . . all your anxieties . . . anyone that you might be concerned about, your family or your friends. Think of any problems that you might have and write them down.

Now fold the paper very gently. Are you sure that you covered everything? Add anything else that might come up, anything that you have not been able to handle.

Fold your paper again and put it in your Godbag. Notice that the Godbag has been designed with two sturdy handles at the top.

Now picture a very large, beautiful balloon. It can be any color that you want it to be. Picture this large balloon over your head . . . up in the sky.

It is a beautiful day and this magnificent balloon is just hanging there above you . . . floating gently above your head . . . just floating . . . waiting for you.

Notice that there is a string hanging from your balloon. The string is tied to the balloon just waiting for you to hold it. See the string just floating there . . . waiting for you to take it in your hand.

Reach up and take the string. Now tie it to the handles of your Godbag. Tie it nice and tight. Now watch the balloon as it floats higher and higher up into the universe. See it floating higher and higher into the sky . . . above the clouds . . .

Watch it get smaller and smaller as it floats higher and higher . . . carrying your Godbag up into the heavens, up into the Powers of the Universe, up into the Powers of your Higher Power . . . God.

Know that it is carrying everything that you have written in your Godbag . . . all your problems . . . all your negative feelings . . . all that you want to turn over to your Higher Power . . . everything that you cannot handle alone.

Know that your balloon is carrying your Godbag up to the Powers of the Universe and you have done everything that you can do right now that is good and right in your life today.

Now feel a tremendous relief as all the weight that you have been carrying on your shoulders is removed as it floats higher and higher to your Higher Power, in your Godbag.

All your fears are being removed as you feel lighter and lighter, knowing that everything is right in the Universe . . . that order and balance is returning to your life as you feel lighter and lighter.

*Know that you are free as "God is doing for you
what you could not do for yourself."**

(*From "The Promises" in **The Big Book,** Alcoholics Anonymous.)

Back To Reality

You can imagine your Godbag anytime and anywhere. It is always
with you. When you come back slowly to the room, know that you
have created something that can always work for you, whenever you
remember it is there.

It is really very helpful to make a real physical Godbag, too. You can
just use a paper bag if you like. Actually take a sheet of paper, write
down what you cannot handle, put it in the Godbag and watch for
miracles.

" ... watch for miracles !"

Personal Prescription
Fifth Week

Date _____

- Continue morning and evening meditation.
- Continue to write your affirmations 10 times a day and reaffirm and visualize them before going to sleep at night.
- Be aware of everything that comes up in your self-talk that is negative and notice how it blocks you from going forth. Record your negative tapes.
- As you bring your attention to the *now* begin to get in touch with your resistance to what you don't like and see what you do with this resistance. Begin to accept whatever comes up as a learning experience.

Commitment

Date _____

I will continue to meditate two times a day.

I am continuing to expand my awareness to all phases of my life as I am learning to live in the now.

I will practice the gift of forgiveness each opportunity that I have.

I will continue to bring my attention to my blocks and write them down as I become aware of them.

Observations

I have made the following new discoveries as a result of this commitment:

Fifth Week Checklist

	Mon	Tues	Wed	Thur	Fri	Sat	Sun
Morning Meditation							
Morning Inspirational Readings							
Visualizations							
Morning Affirmations							
Bringing Attention to My Self-talk							
Bringing Attention to One Routine							
Evening Inspirational Readings							
Evening Meditation							
Visualizations							
Evening Affirmations							

Week 6

Personal Plan For Meditation Plus

Whether you have come to this sixth and final week of *Meditation Plus* in six weeks or more does not matter. Whatever time it has taken you is exactly right for you. You have traveled an exciting yet bumpy journey to get to your new place of awareness.

This week we will look a bit further, smooth out some more of the rough spots, and offer some more exercises for peace and love.

Writing Sixth Week's Experiences

1. How did I respond to the variety of feelings that came up during meditation this week?

2. How did I feel different this week?

3. When I brought my attention to one routine, I . . .

4. When I brought my attention to myself as a *listener* and *talker*, I discovered . . .

5. I accomplished more _____ less _____ same _____ this week.

6. I learned these new things about me . . .

7. I felt better _____ worse _____ same _____ about myself.

8. Important points to remember . . .

Now go on with your own questions . . . exploring . . .thinking . . . re-feeling.

Pause For Reflections

Date _____

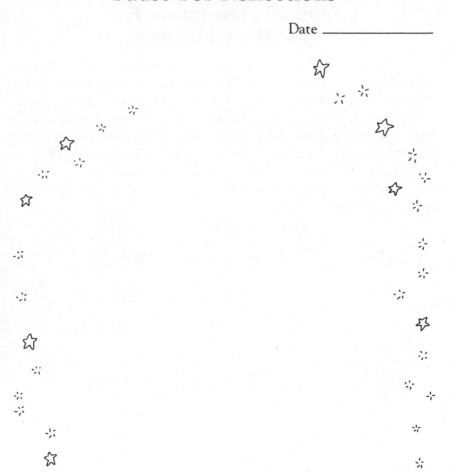

Review Of The Tools

Spiritual Prescriptions For Growth And Change

For the last few weeks you have been learning many healthy positive tools to help you grow, be happy and find your inner truth. You have learned steps so that you no longer need to run away from yourself; so that you can stay and accept and learn to love yourself. Some are simple tools that require simply being with yourself and bringing attention to whatever comes up. Other tools require deeply searching yourself for your truth, for your inner wisdom.

All the tools require only willingness. You will always get what you need if you are willing.

"meditation quiets and clears the mind..."

1. Meditation

Quiets and clears the mind which leads to . . .

2. Awareness And Insight

We begin to see what is between ourselves and God. We begin to shine a light on our stumbling blocks. We can then listen with clarity so that we can hear God's Will for us.

3. Finding Peace In Our Inner Sanctuary

We learn how to go within to find our own peace . . . our own truth.

4. Acceptance

We begin to forgive and accept ourselves so that we can become free from yesterday and tomorrow.

5. Emptying Ourselves

We become empty so that we can refill.

6. Visualize

7. Affirm

We use visualizations and affirmations to create a new positive self-image.

feel the goodness

Doors To The Past And The Future

Here is an exercise that will help you clear up any issues that are still bothering you from your past, or any fears that you still might have about the future.

It would be nice if you could have someone read this to you. If not, just read it over first. It is perfectly fine, as in all these guided imageries, if you open your eyes and read on or record them yourself on a tape and play them back. Relax and spend some time meditating.

Do all that you need to do to bring yourself into your special place.

Call in your inner guide. Know that you are perfectly safe; that nothing can harm you.

Take off your shoes so that you can feel the ground beneath your feet. Smell the air and see if there are any special aromas. Stop a moment and listen. Any special sounds? Feel the breeze on your skin . . . gently blowing across your face and your hair.

Ask her to lead you down your path of your *now*, past your past and your future. See before you a winding, gentle path. Off to the left are many different trails that go into a forest. These lead to the trails of your past. Off to the right are more trails that lead off into a forest. These are the trails of your future.

As you slowly walk along the path of your *now*, are you feeling pulled in any direction, other than straight ahead?

Let her lead you to where you might still have an issue in your past. Walk down that trail to the left . . . moving away the branches that might be in your way as you enter the forest. Step over any rocks and fallen trees . . . careful not to let them scratch you.

Step out into an opening and see what it is that has brought you down this path.

Who do you see?

Is there someone that you have not forgiven . . . someone with whom you are still angry?

Ask your inner guide to help you with whatever needs to be done so that you can be free from your past.

Take all the time that you need.

Come back out to the main path . . . continuing to walk until another side path draws you . . . whether it be to the right or left.

Continue to ask your inner guide for guidance. You will know what needs to be done so that you can be free of your past and your future.

When you feel complete, come back to your own special place and spend some time really feeling good about yourself. Know that you are doing wonderful work in your life today. You are freeing the space within you to let your Higher Power work with you and through you.

Let these good feelings permeate every cell of your body, knowing that you are going to take them back to your consciousness when you come out of your special place. Know that the new space that you have created is being filled with positive energy. Your life is getting lighter and brighter as you move on in your path in your *now*.

Whenever you are ready, return to your room. Be sure to count to five before you open your eyes.

"let these good feelings
permeate every cell of your
body..."

Balance

Many times we may become stuck in one or two areas of our lives and so become blocked from growing in other areas. Or we may devote too much time to an activity, a relationship, a job or any one of a number of obsessions and therefore neglect growing and becoming a more complete person.

Let's take some time to look at some important areas of your life. Look at them with your gentle witness, without judging, with just quiet acceptance.

Here are a few questions to begin your thinking and examining. Remember, this is a time to be gentle with yourself.

Where do I want to grow?

Where is my life going well?

What are my blocks from the past? ·

How is old programming still keeping me stuck?

Add any other questions you can think of here.

Now turn to the next page and examine the different areas of your life. Spend some time meditating and going into your special place. Bring in your inner guide and ask for help and feedback.

Affirmations For Changes

Review your affirmations for changes. Remember to write your own 10 times a day for 21 days for a major change in your life. Say them every morning and every evening before you go to bed. Say them over and over again during the day. Write them on index cards and carry them with you. Write them on stickers and place them at places

family

recreational

spiritual

friends

career

creative

health

financial

"look at them with your gentle witness, without judging, with just quiet acceptance."

where you will see them often. You can use the ones that are appropriate for you at this time. Add your own to the list. Change them when they no longer are needed. Remember, the more that you repeat them, the more they will become a part of your automatic thinking. You are creating new tapes which create new thoughts. You are creating your own reality. Your future is only as positive as the thoughts that you hold in your mind today.

I am worthy of beautiful changes in my life today.

I give myself permission to grow and change.

I give myself permission to do good things for me today.

I am a beautiful person full of healthy needs and feelings, and I can express them freely and openly whenever I choose.

I now have the total intention of letting God work through me.

I am letting myself be charged and directed by my creative energy.

I am letting God flow through my life.

It's okay to feel good about me today.

I am letting God flow through my life.

Now write your own.

This is an exercise that you have already done in this workbook. Review where you are now. See where else you would like to change. See what worked for you before.

"You should constantly picture something better than you are now experiencing."

Catherine Ponder

1. List everything in your life that you really don't want anymore.

2. List everything that you would like to have.

3. Now choose *one* of the things you would like to have out of your life today and make the intention to no longer have it.

   Today I am positively letting go of . . .

   I visualize myself as if this has already occurred . . .

   My affirmation for this expectancy is . . .

   Goal date . . .

4. Now choose *one* of the things you would like to have in your life today and make the intention to have it.

   Today I have a positive expectancy of . . .

I visualize myself as if this has already occurred . . .

My affirmation for this expectancy is . . .

Goal date . . .

Remember . . . you must empty before you can fill. When you are willing to let go of the people, places and things that are destructive or negative in your life today, you will become open to positive changes and additions to take place.

stay with that person and be that person for a while.

Personal Prescription
Sixth Week

Date _____

This is the last week of my workbook but I will continue to practice these tools and others that I will learn as I continue to grow. As the journey is my own, I will design this page as I wish. I know I can change it anytime, add something new or remove anything that is no longer working for me.

Commitment

Date _____

Observations

I have made the following new discoveries as a result of this commitment:

Sixth Week And On Checklist

Read the section on "When It Is Hard To Meditate" and use the affirmations provided so that you will look forward to it, rather than find it a chore. But if you do find it difficult, let those feelings and thoughts be your meditation and notice how you handle such situations. Let it be a learning experience for you.

	Mon	Tues	Wed	Thur	Fri	Sat	Sun
Morning Meditation							
Morning Inspirational Readings							
Visualizations							
Morning Affirmations							
Bringing Attention to My Self-talk							
Bringing Attention to One Routine							
Recording My Blocks							
Forgiveness Affirmations							

(continued)

	Mon	Tues	Wed	Thur	Fri	Sat	Sun
Evening Inspirational Readings							
Evening Meditation							
Visualizations							
Evening Affirmations							
Now Add Your Own							

The Ending That Is
The Beginning

Know that learning goes on forever. Know that even if you think you will not remember what you have learned, these lessons have now become a part of you that will not be forgotten for as long as you continue not to fill your body with harmful drugs and your life with destructive dependencies.

I hope that you will continue to meditate and to use positive affirmations and to believe in yourself. Give yourself abundant time and love and know that you are worth it. Continue to reach within for that special spark so that you can continue to grow in inner peace and self-esteem and closer to your Higher Power.

Now that you have completed Meditation Plus, you are well able to continue your daily meditations, visualizations and affirmations on your own. At some time you might like to join or start a meditation support group. This can be very helpful.

I will be very pleased to hear from you with any comments or suggestions that might be helpful to others.

Thank you for sharing this special time in your life with me!

With Love and Faith,

Ruth

"continue to reach within
for that special spark...
continue to grow in inner
peace..."

Certificate of Achievement

This Acknowledges The Completion Of Six Weeks Of Training

In

Meditation Plus

for

Your Name _____

You are hereby eligible to experience and enjoy all
the unfolding miracles of the universe.
As you continue your practice, the universe will continue to
reward you with its magnificent wonders and gifts
full of love and joy and serenity.
May yours be a beautiful journey of Spirituality and
love, traveled by the brave and rare few. And may you
continue to give to others all that you learn.

Congratulations!

Recommended Reading List

Adult Children of Alcoholics, Janet Woititz, Health Communications, Pompano Beach, Florida, 1983. *New York Times* best seller on subject.*

Affirmations — 21 Day Workshop, Ruth Fishel. A 21-day program designed for your personal use.*

Anatomy of an Illness: As Perceived by the Patient, Norman Cousins. W.W. Norton and Co., Inc., Bantam Edition, 1981. Excellent true story of positive thinking in healing disease.

The Aquarian Conspiracy, Marilyn Ferguson. Moving and inspiring book on the Human Potential and Spiritual Movement in the world today.

The Art of Inner Listening, Jessie K. Crum. RE-QUEST Books, The Theosophical Publishing House, Wheaton, Illinois 60189, 1975. A gentle, spiritual guide to looking within.

Being Peace, Thich Nhat Hanh. Parallax Press, P.O. Box 7355, Berkeley, California 94707, 1987. An important book for the world today, he discusses the importance of being peaceful in order to make peace.

Chop Wood Carry Water, Rick Fields with Peggy Taylor, Rex Weyler and Rick Ingrasci. Jeremy P. Tarcher, Inc., 1984. A Guide to

Finding Spiritual Fulfillment in Everyday Life.*

A Course of Miracles. Three-volume course centering on the need for forgiveness for healing. Extraordinarily inspirational and enlightening.*

Children of Alcoholics, Robert Ackerman. Learning Publications, Holmes Beach, Florida, 1978. Good information for children and adult children of alcoholics.*

Choicemaking, Sharon Wegscheider-Cruse. Health Communications, Pompano Beach, Florida, 1985. Good information for co-dependents and adult children of alcoholics.*

Creative Visualization, Ronald Shone. Thorsons Publishers, Inc., 377 Park Ave. South, New York, NY 10016, 1984.

Creative Visualization, Shakti Gawain. Whatever Publishing, Inc., 1979; Bantam Books Inc., 1982. Clear and easy-to-follow techniques for relaxation, opening energy centers, affirmations, creating and following through with goals, etc.*

Cutting Through Spiritual Materialism, Chogyam Trungpa. Shambhala Publications, Inc., 314 Dartmouth St., Boston, MA 02116, 1987. Helps us look at our tendencies for self-deception and ego-gratification.

Each Day A New Beginning. The Hazelden Foundation, Box 176, Center City, MN 55012, 1982. A wonderful way for women to begin their day. A daily book of inspirational meditations for women in recovery.*

Emmanuel's Book compiled by Pat Rodegast and Judith Stanton. Friends Press, P.O. Box 1006, Weston, CT, 1985. A delightful book full of wisdom on a variety of subjects. A manual for living comfortably in the cosmos.*

From Medication to Meditation, Ruth Fishel, Positives Unlimited, 1985. Gentle introduction to meditation as a useful tool in recovery of addictions.*

Getting Well Again, O. Carl Simonton, Stephanie Mathews-Simonton and James L. Creighton. Bantam Books, Inc., New York, 1978. Highly successful program of healing in cancer which can be adapted for any other illness.

God Makes The Rivers To Flow. Passages for meditation selected by Eknath Easwaran. Nilgiri Press, 1982. An inspiring collection of meditations from all major religions throughout the ages.*

A Gradual Awakening, Steven Levine. Anchor Books, Anchor Press/Doubleday, Garden City, New York, 1979. Gentle and beautifully moving guide to Insight Meditation.*

How Can I Help? Ram Dass and Paul Gorman. Alfred A. Knopf, New York, 1985. This should be a must for everyone in the helping professions and those who are moved to help others in their daily life. Excellent sections on dealing with and avoiding burnout.

I Am That, Swami Muktananda. Syda Foundation, P.O. Box 600, South Fallsburg, New York, 1978. Informative and instructive techniques for breathing and awareness.

Is It Love or Is It Addiction? Brenda Schaeffer. Hazelden, Box 176, Center City, MN 55012, 1987. Excellent insight into addictive behaviors and personalities.*

Journey of Awakening: A Meditator's Guidebook, Ram Dass. Bantam Books, New York, 1985.

The Journey Within: A Spiritual Path to Recovery, Ruth Fishel. Health Communications, Inc., 1721 Blount Road, Pompano Beach, FL 33069, 1987. A unique program for recovery which includes meditation, visualizations and affirmations.*

Learning to Love Yourself, Sharon Wegscheider-Cruse. Health Communicatins, Inc., 1721 Blount Road, Pompano Beach, FL 33069, 1987. Practical steps to helping you improve your self-worth.*

Living in the Light, Shakti Gawain. Whatever Publishing Company, P.O. Box 137, Mill Valley, CA 94942, 1986. Clear, practical guide to learn to trust your intuition and develop creativity.

Love Is Letting Go Of Fear, Gerald G. Jampolsky. Bantam Books, 1981. The founder of the Center for Attitudinal Healing offers simple advice for spiritual growth based on *A Course of Miracles*.*

Meditation, An Eight-point Program, Eknath Easwaran. Blue Mountain Center of Meditation, 1978. Obtained from Nilgiri Press, Box 477, Petaluma, CA 94953. Inspirational. A good place to begin in the morning.*

The Miracle of Mindfulness! Thich Nhat Hanh. Beacon Press, Boston, MA, 1976. A simple, gentle book that teaches Mahayana and Theravada traditions of Buddhist meditation.*

Mother Wit, Diane Mariechild. The Crossing Press, Trumansburg, New York, 1981.

The Myth of Freedom and **The Way of Meditation** by Chogyam Trungpa, Shambhala Publications, Boulder, CO, 1976.

Open Mind, Open Heart, Thomas Keating. Amity House, 106 Newport Bridge Rd., Warwick, N.Y., 1986. Christian-based meditation with step-by-step guidance in centering prayer.

Prospering Woman, Ruth Ross. Whatever Publishing, Inc., 1982. Helps us to discover the negative blocks that keep us from prospering. Use of affirmations and visualizations to turn them around.*

Ramtha, Edited by Steve Lee Weinberg. Sovereignty, Inc., Box 926, Eastsound, WA 98245. While you may not agree with the premise (Ramtha being a warrior from 35,000 years ago, returning today and speaking through the body of another), there is excellent information on the reprogramming of positive tapes, taking responsibility for one's own life and discovering the road to happiness.

Shame and Guilt: Characteristics of the Dependency Cycle. Ernest Kurtz. Hazelden Foundation, 1984.

Teach Only Love, Gerald G. Jampolsky. Bantam, 1983. See description of **Love Is Letting Go Of Fear.***

Twelve Steps and Twelve Traditions. Alcoholics Anonymous World Services, Inc., Box 459, Grand Central Station, New York, NY 10163, 1952. A must for anyone in a recovery program. The basic program for growth and recovery for all programs based on the principles of AA.*

Twenty Four Hours A Day. Hazelden Foundation, Center City, MN 55012, 1954. Especially for recovering alcoholics. A daily meditation book to help begin each day in recovery.*

Way of the Peaceful Warrior, Dan Millman. H.J. Kramer, Inc. P.O. Box 1082, Tiburon, CA 94920, 1980. Unusual! Written as a novel. Contains wisdom and insight. Very refreshing!*

Wellsprings, Anthony de Mello. Image Books, A division of Doubleday & Company, Inc., Garden City, New York, 1986. A beautiful book directing us to experience our senses and feelings through the use of inspirational exercises.

WomanSpirit, Hallie Iglehart. Harper and Row Publishers, San Francisco, 1983.

Working Inside Out, Margo Adair. Wingbow Press, Distributed by People Books, Berkeley, CA 94710, 1984.

The Way Of Zen, Alan W. Watts. Pantheon Books, Inc. 1957.

Zen In The Art Of Archery, Eugene Herrigel. Pantheon Books, Inc., 1953. Vintage Books Edition, 1971.

Zen Mind, Beginner's Mind, Shunryu Suzuki. John Weatherhill, Inc., 7-6-13 Roppongi, Minato-ku, Tokyo 106. An introduction to Zen meditation and practice.*

*Books starred are carried at SERENITY, INC., 89 I Washington Ave., Natick, MA 01760 or can be ordered by writing to SERENITY, INC., P.O. Box 664, Natick, MA 01760, or by calling TOLL FREE 1-800-842-4240 (In Mass. 617-655-7774).

Ruth Fishel

For up-to-date information on Ruth Fishel's workshops, seminars, conferences and tapes or to be on her mailing list, write to:

> Ruth Fishel
> *Spirithaven*
> 19 Chappaquiddick Rd.
> Centerville, MA 02632

The following tapes are now available:

You Cannot Meditate Wrong .... $ 9.00

Time For Joy! $10.00

Transforming Your Past Into Presents
Finding Your Own Special Gifts .... $ 9.00

Guided Exercises For Deepening Your
Meditation Experience .... $ 9.00

The Journey Within .... $ 9.00

Discovering Your Source Of Peace With
The Powerful Tool Of Noting .... $ 9.00

Other Health Communications Publications By Ruth Fishel

5 Minutes For World Peace . . . Forever:
A 90 Day Affirmation Plan .... $ 4.95

Time For Joy: Daily Affirmations .... $ 6.95

The Journey Within:
A Spiritual Path To Recovery .... $ 8.95

Learning To Live In The Now:
6-Week Personal Plan To Recovery .... $ 8.95

If you enjoyed this book . . .

Other Books in This Series

THE JOURNEY WITHIN: A Spiritual Path to Recovery
by Ruth Fishel.
ISBN 0-932194-41-9   **$8.95**

This book will lead you from your dysfunctional beginnings to
the place within where renewal occurs.

GENESIS: Spirituality in Recovery for Co-dependents
by Julie D. Bowden and Herbert L. Gravitz.
ISBN 0-932194-56-7   **$6.95**

A self-help spiritual program for adult children of trauma, an
in depth look at "turning it over" and "letting go".

GIFTS FOR PERSONAL GROWTH AND RECOVERY
by Wayne Kritsberg
ISBN 0-932194-60-5   **$6.95**

Gifts for healing, which include journal writing, breath
control and bonding.